HOMES, AND HOW
TO MAKE THEM

PREFACE.

These letters between the architect and his friends are composed of hints and suggestions relating to the building of homes. Their aim is to give practical information to those about to build, and to strengthen the growing demand for better and truer work.

Even those who are not yet ready to build for themselves are seldom without an instinctive longing to do so at some future time, and a lively concern in the present achievements of their friends and neighbors, in this direction. Such will, I trust, find something interesting and instructive in these pages, and be moved thereby to a more cordial hatred of whatever is false and useless, and love for the simple and true.

E.C.G.
SPRINGFIELD, March, 1874.

CONTENTS

LIST OF ILLUSTRATIONS.

IN LETTERS BETWEEN AN ARCHITECT
AND A FAMILY MAN SEEKING A HOME.

ONLY ONE CORNER

LETTER I.

From the Architect.

EVERY MAN SHOULD HAVE A HOME.

My Dear John:

Now that your "ship" is at last approaching the harbor, I am confident your first demonstration in honor of its arrival will be building yourself a house; exchanging your charmingly good-for-nothing air-castle for an actual flesh-and-blood, matter-of-fact dwelling-house, two-storied and French-roofed it may be, with all the modern improvements. In many respects, you will find the real house far less satisfactory and more perplexing than the creation of your fancy. Air-castles have some splendid qualities. There are no masons' and carpenters' contracts to be made, no plumbers' bills to be vexed over, the furnaces never smoke, and the water-pipes never freeze; they need no insurance, and you have no vain regrets over mistakes in your plans, for you may have alterations and additions whenever you please without making a small pandemonium and eating dust and ashes while they are in process. Nevertheless, I have no doubt you will plunge at once into the mysteries and miseries of building, and, knowing your inexperience, I cannot at such a juncture leave you wholly to your own devices.

It is a solemn thing to build even the outside of a house. You not only influence your fellow-men, but reveal your own character; for houses have a facial expression as marked as that of human beings, often strangely like their owners, and, in most cases, far more lasting. Some destroy your faith in human nature, and give you an ague chill when you pass them; others look impudently defiant, while many make you cry out, "Vanity of vanities!" If you are disposed to investigate the matter, you will find that the history of nations may be clearly traced in the visible moral expression of the homes of the people;—in the portable home-tents of the Arabs; the homely solidity of the houses in Germany and Holland; the cheerful, wide-spreading hospitality of Switzerland; the superficial elegance and extravagance of France; the thoroughness and self-assertion of the English; and in the heterogeneous conglomerations of America, made up of importations from every land and nation under the sun,—a constant striving and changing,—a mass of problems yet unsolved.

A friend once said to me while we were passing an incurably ugly house, "The man who built that must have had a very good excuse for it!" It was a profound remark, but if that particular building were the only one needing apology for its ugliness, or if there were no common faults of construction and interior arrangement, I should not think you in special need of warning or counsel from me. There are, however, so many ill-looking and badly contrived houses, so few really tasteful ones, while year after year it costs more and more to provide the comfortable and convenient home which every man wants and needs for himself and family, that I am sure you will be grateful for any help I may be able to give you.

We are told that all men, women, and children ought to be healthy, handsome, and happy. I have strong convictions that every man should also have a home, healthful, happy, and beautiful; that it is a right, a duty, and therefore a possibility. Small and humble it may be, cheap as to cost, but secure, refined, full of conveniences, and the dearest spot on earth, a home of his own.

In the hope of making the way to this joyful consummation easier and plainer for you, I propose to give you a variety of hints, information, and illustrations relating to your undertaking, and will try to make my practical suggestions so well worth your attention that you shall not overlook what I may say upon general principles. There is a right and a wrong way of doing almost everything. I am yours, for the right way.

LETTER II.

From John.

A GRATEFUL CLIENT.

MY DEAR ARCHITECT: How did you know my ship was coming in? Queer, isn't it, that when a man does get a few stamps, his friends all find it out, and can tell him just what he ought to do with them. But you're right. I've lived in an air-castle long enough. It's altogether too airy for cold weather, and a house of my own I'm bound to have. Your information and advice will be exactly in order; for it is a fact, that, until a man has built at least one house for himself, he is as ignorant as the babe unborn, not only of how to do it, but, what is ten times worse, ignorant of what he wants to do. So go ahead by all means; make a missionary of yourself for my benefit. Don't get on your high heels too soon, and undertake to tell me what won't be of the slightest use unless I have a fortune to expend.

MRS. AND MRS. JOHN

Give me something commonplace and practical, something that I can apply to a "villa" of two rooms if my ship happens to be empty. I suppose it's all true that an ugly-looking house is a sign of want of wit rather than want of money, but there are lots of people who haven't either, precious few that have both. At all events, the man who has only one thousand dollars to spend is just as anxious to spend it to the best advantage as he who has five thousand or fifty.

Mrs. John is delighted. She is bent on the new house, but knows I shall get everything wrong end first from cellar to attic. I always supposed a good kitchen was a desirable part of a family establishment, but the chief end of her plans is bay-windows and folding doors. However, if you tell us to put the front door at the back side of the house, or do any other absurd thing, it will be all right.

As to your preachment on general principles, I'll do the best I can with it; but don't give me too much at once.

Yours,
JOHN.

LETTER III.

From the Architect.

THE BEAUTY OF TRUTH AND UTILITY.

Dear John: I am glad my efforts in your behalf are likely to be appreciated, especially if you share this common opinion of architects, that their mission is accomplished when they have made a pretty picture, and that they are an expensive luxury, which the man who would build himself a house must forego if he would be able to finish. Greater durability, comfort, and convenience are not expected on account of their assistance, only that the house shall be more surprisingly beautiful. Doubtless there is some ground for this poor opinion, but the architects are not alone in their folly, or wholly responsible; they attempt to supply an unreasonable demand, and are driven to employ unworthy means.

The first grand lesson for you to learn (you must have patience with a little more "preachment") is that the beauty of your building cannot be thrust upon it, but must be born with it, must be an inseparable part of it, the result and evidence of its real worth. We must forget our great anxiety as to how our houses shall be clothed, aiming first to make them strong and durable, comfortable and convenient, being morally certain that they will not then be disagreeable to look upon. Professing a great contempt for a man who tries to seem something better and wiser than he is, let us be equally severe in condemning every building that puts on airs and boldly bids us admire what is only fit to be despised. The pendulum seems to have swung away from the plain, utilitarian mode of building that was forced upon our ancestors by a stern necessity,— possibly chosen from a sense of duty,—to the other extreme; giving us, instead of the old-time simplicity, many a fantastic design that claims admiration for its originality or its modern style. The notion that there can be a mere architectural fashion, having any rights that intelligent people are bound to respect, is quite absurd. Improved modes of construction and new helps to comfort and convenience are constantly invented, but one might as well talk of the latest fashions for the lilies of the fields or the stars in the heavens, as of a fashionable style in architecture or any other enduring work of art. Whatever building is nobly and enduringly useful, thoroughly adapted to its uses, cannot be uncomely. Its outward beauty may be increased by well-contrived disposition of materials, or even added details not strictly essential to its structure; but, if rightly built, it will not be ugly without these additions, and beware of using them carelessly. What might have been a very gem of homely and picturesque grace, if left in modest plainness, may be so overburdened with worthless trash that its original expression is lost and its simple beauty becomes obtrusive deformity. Even conspicuous cheapness is not necessarily unpleasant to see, but don't try to conceal it by forcing the materials to seem something better than they are. Let wood stand for wood, brick for brick, and never ask us to imagine a brown-stone value to painted sheet-iron. There is, too, a deeper honesty than mere truth-telling in material; a conscientiousness of purpose, an artistic spiritual sense of the eternal fitness, without which there can be no worthy achievement, no lasting beauty.

Accepting this doctrine, which cannot be too often or too strongly urged, although it is not new,—indeed, it is old as the universe,—you will, I think, be puzzled to find an excuse for yourself if you disfigure a charming landscape or a village street by an uncouth building. Build plainly if you will, cheaply if you must, but, by all that is fair to look upon or pleasant to the thought, be honest. It will require some study and much courage, but verily you will have your reward, and I for one shall be proud to write myself your admiring friend.

LETTER IV.

From John.

PROFESSIONAL FOLLY.

My Dear Architect: I've been trying to learn my "first grand lesson," as laid down in your second epistle to yours truly. About all I can make of it is: Firstly, that my house is for myself to live in,—wife and babies included,—not for my neighbors to look at; and, secondly, that however much I may try to humbug my fellow-sinners in other ways, I'm not to build a lie into my house, where it is sure to be found out, after I'm dead and gone, if not before.

You wonder what my opinion is of architects. Well, without being personal, I'm free to maintain that as a rule I'm afraid of 'em. The truth is, they don't care what a fellow's house costs him, whatever they may say in the beginning; and I never knew a man to build from an architect's plans that his bills didn't come in just about double what he laid out for. They want to get up a grand display, if it's a possible thing, so everybody that comes along will stop and say, "What a charming house! Who made the plans?" while from beginning to end it may be all for show and nothing for use, and mortgaged to the very chimney-tops. That's my opinion, and I'm not alone in it, either.

There was my neighbor down the road,—he wanted a commonish kind of a house. Nothing would do but his wife must have it planned by a "professional" man. Result was, she had to put her best bedstead square in the middle of the room, and there was no possible place for the sitting-room lounge but to stand it on end behind a door in the corner. Another acquaintance of mine had $5,000. Didn't want to spend a cent more than that. Called on an architect,—may have been you, for all I know; architect made sketches, added here a little and there a good deal, made one or two rooms a few feet bigger, poked the roof up several feet higher, and piled the agony on to the outside, until, when the thing was done, it cost him $11,000! Of course it ran him into debt, and most likely will be sold at auction. He'll never get what it cost him, unless he can sell it as we boys used to swap wallets,—without looking at the inside. But everybody says it's "lovely," and wants to know who was his architect.

That, I expect, is just where the shoe pinches. If an architect can only make a fine show with another man's money, he gets a reputation in no time; but if he has a little conscience, and tries to plan a house that can be built for a given sum, every one says it looks cheap, no kind of taste, and very likely the owner himself is grouty about it, and next time goes for another man.

I don't envy you a bit. But don't be discouraged.

Yours,
JOHN.

26

LETTER V.

From the Architect.

BUILDING-SITES
AND FOUNDATION-WALLS.

DEAR JOHN: You seem to have made as much of my last letter as could reasonably be expected. I might reply to your unfortunate experience with architects, by describing the cost and annoyance of the subsequent alterations, almost inevitable whenever a house is built without carefully studied plans; and I do assure you that when the cost of a house exceeds the owner's estimates, it is simply because he does not know his own mind beforehand, or stupidly fails to have his plans and contracts completed before he begins to build. It's no more the fault of the architect than of the man in the moon. By and by you shall have a chapter on the whole duty of architects, as I understand it, but not until I have given you something more practical to think of and possibly to work upon.

Nothing astonishes me more than the absurdly chosen sites of many rural and suburban dwellings, unless it is the dwellings themselves. Notwithstanding our great resources in this respect, all considerations, not only of good taste and landscape effect, but even of comfort and convenience, are often wholly ignored. For the most trivial reasons, houses are erected in such locations and of such shapes as to be forever in discord with their surroundings,—a perpetual annoyance to beholders and discomfort to their occupants. I will not at present pursue the subject, but shall assume that the ground whereon your house will stand is at least firm and dry; if it isn't, no matter how soon it falls, it won't be fit to live in. Any preparation for the foundation in the way of puddling or under-draining will then be quite superfluous.

Unless you are obliged to economize to the uttermost, let your cellar extend under the whole house, and make it of good depth, not less than 7-1/2 feet,—8-1/2 is better. When this is ready, I suppose you will start for the nearest ledge, and bring the largest rocks that can be loosened by powder or dragged by oxen, and set them in solemn array around the cellar, their most smiling faces turned inward. If you can find huge flat stones of one or two yards area, and six to twelve inches thick, you will feel especially fortunate. In either case you will survey these with admiration, and rejoice in thinking that, though the rains may fall, and the floods and the winds beat upon it, your house will rest on its massive support in absolute security, never showing the ugly cracks and other signs of weakness that spring from imperfect foundations. Perhaps not, but it will be far more likely to do so than if the first course of stones in the bed of gravel or hard pan are no larger than you can easily lift. You cannot give these huge bowlders such firm resting-place as they have found for themselves in the ages since they were dropped by the dissolving glaciers. However you handle them, there will be cavities underneath, where the stone does not bear upon the solid ground. The smaller ones you may rub or pound down till every inch of the motherly bosom shall feel their pressure. Upon this first course of—pebbles, if you please, lay larger ones that shall overlap and bind them together, using mortar if you wish entire solidity. As the wall rises, introduce enough of large size to bind the whole thoroughly. Above the footing the imperfect bearings of the larger stones are of less consequence, since there is little danger of their crushing one another.

28

ROUGH STRENGTH AND SMOOTH-FACED WEAKNESS

I say you will probably set their smooth faces inward, where they can be seen, which is quite natural and well enough, provided this is not their only merit. If behind there is a lame and impotent conclusion, a tapering point on which it is impossible to build without depending upon the bank of earth, it will be better to have less beauty and more strength. I don't like a foundation wall that is "backed up"; it should be solid quite through; if any difference, let it be in favor of the back or outside. You will find plenty of walls bulging into the cellar, not one crowding outward.

If the footing of a foundation is made as it should be, the upper part may be much thinner, since there is no danger of crushing it by any probable weight of building. It may be crowded inward by the pressure of surrounding earth, especially if the building is of wood. To guard against this, interior buttresses of brick, or partition walls in the cellar, will perhaps cost less than a thicker main wall. The buttresses you may utilize by making them receive shelves, support the sides of the coal-bin, etc., while the partitions will take the place of piers, and, if well laid, need be in smaller houses but four inches thick.

Should your cellar happen to be in a gravelly knoll,—you are thrice and four times blessed if it is,—and if there is a stony pasture near it or a quarry from which you can get the chips, you may try a concrete wall of small stones, gravel, and cement. It will be strong and durable; with a wheelbarrow you can make it yourself if you choose, and the rats will despise it.

Whether your house is one story or ten, built of pine or granite, you can have no better foundation than good hard brick laid in cement mortar; cellular above the footing, as brick walls should usually be made. Between this and stone it will be then a question of economy to be determined by local circumstances.

The details and accessories of cellars, their floors, ventilation, and various conveniences, belong to the interior equipments. There is, however, one point that even precedes the foundation,—the altitude. As the question commonly runs, "How high shall the top of the underpinning be?" Of course this can only be given on an actual site. It is unfortunate to plant a house so low in the ground that its cellar forms a sort of cesspool for the surrounding basin; most absurd to set it up on a stilted underpinning until it looks like a Western gatepost, lifted every year a few inches out of the ground by the frost, till it finally topples over and has to be set anew. Two things you will notice in locating your house,—as soon as the walls and roof are raised, the distance to the street in front will seem to be diminished, and the ground on which the building stands will appear lower than before, lower than you expected or desired. There is so much said and sung about houses being set too low, that it is quite common to find them pushed out of the ground, cellar and all, as though this would atone for a want of elevation in the land itself. There is little danger that you will place your house too high, great danger that you will not raise the earth around it high enough. Be sure that after grading there shall be an ample slope away from the walls; but whether you will have a "high stoop," or pass from the dooryard walk to the porch and thence to the front hall by a single step, will depend upon the character of the house and its surroundings. To express a generous hospitality the main entrance should be so convenient and inviting that it seems easier to enter than to pass the door. This effect, especially in large rambling houses, is most easily obtained by keeping the first floor near the ground. That hospitality and good cheer will always be found beneath your roof is my earnest wish.

LETTER VI.

From John.

GRAVEL-BANKS AND QUAGMIRES.

MY DEAR ARCHITECT: I'm all right on the gravel question. You don't catch me building in anybody's quagmire. There's plenty of rheumatism and fever 'n' ague lying around loose without digging for 'em, and then building a house over the hole to keep 'em in. I don't want to say anything against any man's building-lots, but how in the light of common-sense a man can, with his eyes open, build his shanty on some of the streets in your enterprising city, is too much for my understanding. If they would first put in good big sewers, running slick and clean to the river, and underdrain the whole premises, 't wouldn't be quite so bad. But I don't want them, anyway; give me the high land and the dry land. I'm not particular about founding on a rock, either; that was well enough in old times when they didn't want cellars, but let me have a good bed of sand or gravel. Cellar may not be quite so cool, but all we need is to go down a little deeper, while, as for health, I'd rather be ten feet under ground in such a spot than occupy the "second-story front," in some places I could mention.

Your foundation is all right in theory, and if I was going to put up a steam chimney, a government building, or anything else that must be done in the best way, regardless of expense, I should go for it. For cheap, common work, 't isn't worth while to be over-nice or over-wise. I tell you, there is danger of knowing too much about some things. According to your notion, a man couldn't do better than to stick the ground full of tenpenny nails to start with, and I should think a thousand-legged worm would be about the most substantial animal that treads the globe.

As to planting my house, when I've bought the lot, I'll ask you to take a look at it. I have a fancy for some sort of a sidehill, so I can get into my house, from one side at least, without going up stairs out of doors, and still have the first floor airy and dry.

Yours,
JOHN.

LETTER VII.

From the Architect.

NATURE'S BRICKS ARE BETTER THAN OURS.

DEAR JOHN: Where to build your house may be, in truth, a question quite as important as how to build it. I regret my inability to give you the advice you need. Dr. Bowditch has, I think, intimated that there is an elysian field not far from here of such rare sanitary virtue that if its locality were known there would scarcely be standing-room within its borders for those who would flock thither, or something to that effect. I trust we shall some time have a scientific practical investigation of the whole matter, and such definite information as will enable us at least to qualify, by artificial means, evils that cannot, in thickly settled regions, be wholly avoided. Meantime stick to your text, keep high and dry. If you are bound to have a sidehill, and can find none to suit, you can doubtless make one of the earth thrown from the cellar wherever you locate.

Have you decided what materials to use, whether wood, brick, or stone? You will hardly use any other. Glass houses are not popular, although for their sunlight they ought to be; paper ones are not yet introduced among us,—I'm expecting them every year; and iron, important and useful as it is, and destined to become more so, is not adapted to such buildings as yours. Wood, brick, or stone, then,—which of the three? To spare you all possible confusion, we will take them separately and in order, beginning with the hardest.

For rural dwellings in New England stone is rarely used, except for foundations below ground, being, according to the common notion, better for that purpose than brick, but not as worthy to be seen, unless hammered and chiselled into straight lines and smooth surfaces. Errors both. Well-burned brick laid in cement mortar are nearly always as good as a stone foundation, while nothing can be more effective in appearance than a well-laid wall of native, undressed stone. We have too long neglected one of the most available of our resources in not making use of the small loose stones that abound in many localities. They are cheaper and better than bricks, and, rightly used, so thoroughly in harmony with the nature around them that we should find them in common use if men were half as wise in accepting the means of grace provided for them as they are prone to seek out many inventions. The earlier farmers with enormous industry built them into fences, and then added a second story of wood to keep the sheep from walking over them, or piled them up in conical heaps, watch-towers for the woodchucks. The later farmers, with less patience but possibly more enterprise, are running away from them to the smoother fields and richer mould of the Western prairies. We can do better than either; for, wherever found, they may be used most favorably, not only for foundation walls that are deeply hidden from mortal view, but for the main walls of the entire building,—favorably, not only in point of economy and strength, but with most admirable result as to external appearance. And here you touch your fundamental principle, that the best outward effect can only be obtained by a judicious use of the materials with which you build. You must not make the walls without any reference to their composition or proportions, and then try to conceal the poverty and awkwardness of the structure by pinning up preposterous window-caps, hanging horrible brackets under the eaves that must always be in doubt whether they support the cornice or are supported by it, fixing fantastic verge-boards to the gables, and covering the roof with wooden knick-knacks that mock consistency and defy description. Look rather to the materials at your command, and, whatever they may be, try to dispose them in such way that, while each part performs a legitimate, necessary service, you shall still have variety and harmony.

Because I have suggested building your main walls of natural undressed stone, you must not attempt to construct them of that alone. The main corners, the door and window jambs, the caps and sills, cannot well be made of these rough hard heads and cobbles that are scattered over the fields, or from quarry chips. And here will arise the question of cost. It would seem decidedly grand to use for the corners substantial blocks of hewn stone,—sandstone, granite, marble, or porphyry,—channelled and chamfered, rock-faced, tooled, rubbed, or decorated; key-stones and voussoirs embellished with your monogram or enriched by any other charming device you choose to invent; bands of encaustic tile, brilliant in color and pattern, belts of sculptured stone, and historic tablets,—if you fancy and can afford them. Unless your ship is heavily freighted with Australian gold or African diamonds, by all means dispense with the cut stone, and use brick for the corners, caps, and jambs, and some good flag-stones broken into strips of suitable width and thickness for the sills and belt-courses. This will give you a contrast in color (unless you have the reddest of red sandstone for the walls), the utmost economy and durability of construction, and a whole effect very likely better than that of the stone. These brick dressings may be light, especially the jambs; but the corners, at least, should be laid in such fashion as to bind well into the stone walls, and if of considerable height, should be strengthened by belts of stone, or iron anchors running through the brick and extending into the main wall several feet each way. Any large blank surface may be relieved by a little ingenuity in the selection of the stones for the main walls, introducing, perhaps, some of regular shapes and size, the raised mortar, which may be colored dark or red, marking the joints, or inserting a belt of different color. Horizontal bands of brick laid in fancy pattern may be convenient and effective.

Of course you will not adopt this style of wall unless there is a crop of suitable stones within easy distance. It is more probable that you will be afraid to use what you have than that there are none to use. Whatever can be made into a stone fence will make the walls of a house, if you are not too ambitious of height, and do not attempt to make them too thin. Other things being equal, the thicker the walls, within certain limits, the better. You don't care to build a Bastile, but deep window-jambs without and within add wonderful richness and dignity. If the walls cost little or no more, as is often the case, it is a pity to refuse the additional ground required for their extra thickness. Such walls should not be monopolized by hundred-thousand-dollar churches and fancy summer residences. They are quite suitable for the simplest, most unpretending country homes.

STONE BODY WITH BRICK MEMBERS

You will understand the general idea thus far by the accompanying sketches, with which I must close this letter, without concluding the subject.

LETTER VIII.

From John.

THERE IS A SOFT SIDE EVEN TO
A STONE WALL.

MY DEAR ARCHITECT: I'm slowly digesting your last production; not being an ostrich, it goes rather hard. For all that, it may be worth thinking of. Perhaps I shall be converted by the time the subject is fully shown up. I suppose we've always looked upon these loose rocks and stones sprinkled about the country as a part of the original curse, and have never thought of turning them to any sensible use, though good old Dr. Hopkins seemed to have faith that their soft side would some time be discovered. Funny, isn't it, that we should burn so much fuel and spend so much labor making bricks and other artificial building-blocks, when there are piles of them ready made, that would only cost the hauling? Not always on the square, to be sure, although in some places the ground is full and running over with flat stones that can be laid up as easily as shingles. They would hardly need any mortar, and the brick trimmings you describe would be a nuisance, except for looks. Miles and miles of stone-walls you will see, up and down hillsides and across pastures that don't look worth their taxes. Once in a while the lower half of a cider-mill, the back side of a barn-yard shed, or something of that sort, is made of them; but the people in these parts seem to think it would be folly to use them for anything more dignified. I suppose, because they are too simple and natural,—just as the Almighty made them.

These square-cornered, flat-sided fellows are not the commonest kind, however; and I'm free to maintain that I don't want to build my house more than seventy-five feet high of the smooth cobbles that will scarcely hang together in a respectable stone-heap. I should expect the whole thing would come tumbling down some rainy night.

Mrs. John don't take to the notion of a stone house—not yet. Says they 're wofully old-fashioned and poky,—look like Canadians and poor folks. I just keep still and let her talk,—it's the best way.

Won't such walls be cold and damp? How am I to know whether the stones that I can find are fit to use? Send you a boxful by express?

Yours,
JOHN.

LETTER IX.

From the Architect.

A BROAD HOUSE IS BETTER THAN A HIGH ONE.

MY DEAR JOHN: It will not be necessary for you to send me a stone-heap or a section of pasture-wall for inspection. I would rather venture an opinion from your description.

Of course, these walls alone, if solid, as they doubtless must be, will be cold and damp; they must be furred off within to prevent moisture from condensing on the walls of the rooms. This furring should be done with light studs, secured to the floor timbers above and below, having no connection with the stone walls, the inside of which may be left quite rough, whatever the "builders in the elder days of art" might say to such negligence. For greater permanence and security against fire, instead of wood furrings you may build a lining of brick, leaving an air space of several inches between it and the stone, very much in the same way as if the whole were of brick.

You say you would prefer not to build walls as high as a church tower of smooth cobblestones. Don't; it wouldn't be wise. Still I have seen them, of more humble dimensions, laid in good cement, as such walls always should be laid, that seem as firm as unbroken granite. But you will remember I only advise this mode of building on the condition that you are not ambitious of height. If you are, by all means curb your aspirations, or else buy a city house six or seven stories in the air, where you can gratify your passion for going up and down stairs. There is the best reason in the world why a tall house in the country should look grim, gaunt, and awkward; it is thoroughly inconvenient and out of place. The area of arable land covered by human habitations does not yet interfere with agricultural products. So let us spread ourselves freely. When we have learned the beauty and the strength of co-operation for mutual helpfulness, we shall see the prevailing mode of constructing houses in cities very much modified. Now they stand as books are placed on their shelves,—vertically and edgewise. They would hold just as many people, and be far more convenient, if they could be laid horizontally, one above the other.

BREADTH AND HEIGHT

True, this would involve floors impervious to sound, and fire-proof,— by no means a fatal objection. Since we can neither "fly nor go" in the air, like birds and angels, it is well for us, having found our appropriate level, to abide thereon as far as may be. There is no doubt that where dwellings must be built compactly in "blocks," as we call them, the "flat" arrangement, each tenement being complete on one floor, is the cheapest and best. Even the fourth story in such a building is preferable to a house of eight or ten rooms, two on each floor. But this does not concern you, unless you have a few thousands to invest in tenement-houses. In the right place I like an old-fashioned one-story house, but most people have a prejudice against anything so unpretending.

One other fact besides the worth of co-operation I hope the dwellers in cities will learn to recognize practically. When there were no swift and screaming locomotives, no cosey and comfortable horse-cars, no red and yellow omnibuses even, there was good reason why men must forego the boon of country air; must forget the color of the ground, the smell of the green things growing, and the shape of the heavens above them. But the reason no longer exists. Doubtless the business of a city should be as compact as possible; but for its dwellings, every consideration of comfort and happiness, of physical and moral well-being, demands that the inhabitants shall make the most of their migratory resources and—scatter; find room to build, not tenements or residences, but *homes* for themselves and their children. In the old time safety was found by crowding together within mural walls. Now the case is reversed. Where the population is densest, temptations and dangers do most abound. We've outgrown the walls, let us overcome the evils that were bred within them.

There may be a prejudice against another quality of these stone walls. They are rough. Roughness means want of culture and labor; that implies want of money, and that is—unpardonable. But roughness does not mean any such thing. What are mouldings and frets and carvings but a roughening of otherwise smooth surfaces? Artists of all kinds seek to remove even the appearance of an unbroken plane, and nature abhors a flat exterior, never allows one, even in the most plastic material, if it can be broken. See the waves of the ocean, the mimic billows on a snow-covered plain, the rugged grandeur of the everlasting hills. Fancy a pine, an oak, or an elm tree with trunk and limbs smoothly polished! What if the outside of your walls are somewhat uneven? Let them be so. The shadows will be all the richer, the vines will cling more closely, and maybe the birds will hang their nests in some sunny corner. Do not, then, try to improve the natural faces of the stones with pick and hammer; you will find it hard work, and, very likely, worse than thrown away.

I think you will like, both in exterior effect and in practical result, the plan of building the walls of the first story of stone with brick dressings, as described in my last letter, making the remainder of the house of wood, be the same more or less. If the sketches I send you do not make you in love with this style, or if you do not like to risk the experiment, examine something already built before deciding against it. But first explore the country around you and see if the stony prospect is good.

SECOND STORY OF WOOD

Mr. Donald G. Mitchell not only writes in favor of this mode of building, but proves his faith by his work; his new house at Edgewood being an admirable specimen of it. You will find, too, some noteworthy examples at Newport, for which, with much else in the way of applying a refined taste to rural affairs, we are indebted, directly or indirectly, to the same well-known writer. If, after the pictures, Mrs. John is still doubtful of the result, the examples above mentioned will certainly allay her misgivings.

You must not think I would recommend this as a universal fashion, even where the materials are abundant, but give it place according to its merit.

I hope you will be spared the folly of building your house of dressed stone of uniform size and color, lest it be mistaken for a large tomb or a small jail. That you may not at present be compelled to take up your abode in either, is my sincere wish.

LETTER X.

From John.

TROUT BROOKS ARE BETTER THAN STREET SEWERS.

My dear architect: We read, we saw, and—were conquered. The pictures, the arguments, and especially the illustrious examples, brought down the house, or rather brought it up. Mrs. John is not only fully reconciled to stone walls, but she is decidedly unreconciled to any other,—that is, for the first story; the second story is to be of wood, the walls shingled or slated instead of being covered with clapboards, in the orthodox fashion. She is delighted with the notion that her "Baltimore belles" and the like can clamber against the house without being torn away every two or three years for paint. On the strength of this notion, she has already ordered a big lot of all sorts of herbs and creeping things, from grape-vines and English ivy to sweet-peas and passion-flowers. That's only one thing. Every time we go out to ride she gathers up from the wayside such a load of small rocks as makes the buggy-springs ache. We found a smooth round stone, yesterday, that looks so much like my head she declares it must be a fossil, and is bound to have it set over the front door instead of a monogram. We follow your lead in another direction; if we can't rise in the world without going up stairs for it, we'll try to cultivate the meek and lowly style.

Your best point, according to my thinking, is on the migration question. I read that paragraph over twice, and stuck a pin at the end of it. It doesn't concern me, to be sure; but I have the utmost pity for a man who is content to live all his life shut in between brick walls. To undertake to bring up a family of boys and girls where all the blessed freedom of out-door life is denied them, is worse than pitiful,—it's heathenish. Not that every boy ought to live on a farm and work in a barn-yard,—hoe corn all summer and chop wood all winter,—but I don't believe a child can grow up strong, healthy, and natural, body-wise and soul-wise, unless he has a chance to scrape an acquaintance with Mother Nature with his own hands. When I stake out John City it will be a city of magnificent distances, in the form of a Greek cross,—two wide streets crossing each other at right angles in the middle; all the business at the "four corners," where there will be plenty of short cross streets; the dwellings stretching away for miles on the two broad avenues; house-lots one to ten acres; Union Pacific Railroad will cut through the centre corner-wise; and the Metropolitan Transportation Company, or something else with a big name, will run elegant cars like shuttles through the two main streets, and Mrs. A at the West End can call on Mrs. B at the North, South, or East End, ten miles away, with less trouble than you in your city can go from Salem to Howard Street.

Similarly, Springfield ought to stretch from Longmeadow to Chicopee Street, from Indian Orchard to Agawam. At all events, if your folks will make the most of their opportunities, it will some day be one of the most charming inland cities on the continent. Whether there is good sense, public spirit, and patriotism enough to make it so remains to be seen.

Yours,
JOHN.

LETTER XI.

From the Architect.

THE STRENGTH AND DURABILITY OF BRICK.

My dear John: It is encouraging to know that my suggestions find some favor in your sight. Pray don't go too fast. It isn't well to make up our minds fully until we have heard all sides, lest we have them to unmake, which is always more or less painful.

Notwithstanding the peculiar merits of the stone walls, the coming house,—the house that is to embody all the comforts and amenities of civilized life,—the house of safe and economic construction, well warmed, well ventilated, defiant alike of flood, frosty and fire,—the millennial house, if you please, will doubtless be a brick one. Don't be alarmed. I know just what vision rises before your mind's eye as you read this. A huge square edifice; windows very high from the ground, not very large, square tops, frame and sash painted white; expressionless roof; flat, helpless chimneys perched upon the outer walls, the course of their flues showing in a crooked stain; at the back side a most humiliated-looking wooden attachment, somewhat unhinged as to its doors and out at the elbows as to its windows, evidently hiding behind the pile of brick and mortar that tries to look dignified and grand, but only succeeds in making a great red blot on the landscape; all the while you know the only homelike portion of the establishment is in the wooden rear part. The front rooms are dark and gloomy, the paper hangings are mouldy, the closets musty and damp; there is a combined smell of creosote and whitewash pervading the chambers, and the ceilings hang low. I don't wonder you object to a brick house in the country. Yet, if you propose to build a model, honest and permanent, a house that shall be worth what it costs and look as good as it is, I shall still recommend brick. The growing scarcity of wood, the usual costliness of stone, the abundance of clay, the rapidity with which brick can be made and used,—one season being sufficient to develop the most awkward hod-carrier into a four-dollars-a-day journeyman bricklayer,—the demand for more permanence in our domestic dwellings, and the known worth of brick in point of durability and safety,—all these reasons will, I think, cause a steady increase in their use. Hence it behooves us to study the matter carefully, and see whether any good thing can be done with them.

Since the time, long ago, when the aspiring sons of Noah said to one another, "Go to; let us make brick and burn them thoroughly," to the latest kiln in Hampden brick-yard, there seems to have been little variety in the making or using of them, except that among different nations they have assumed different forms. They are found as huge blocks a foot and a half square, and in little flinty cakes no bigger than a snuff-box. The Romans made the best ones, some of their buildings having defied the elements for seventeen centuries, and their mantle, as to brickmaking, has fallen upon the Dutch. They were found among the ancient Peruvians, and the Chinese made beautiful the outside of the temple by giving a porcelain finish to the brick. Still I fancy they have always been more famous for their use than for their beauty; but their utility is beyond all question. If our modern experience doesn't prove it, read this inscription from an ancient brick pyramid of Howara:—

"Do not undervalue me by comparing me with pyramids of stone; for I am better than they as Jove exceeds the other deities. I am made of bricks from clay, brought up from the bottom of the lake adhering to poles."

Notwithstanding these claims to veneration, there is but little poetry about them, and therefore, I suppose, but little progress. Compared with other materials, they have undergone slight changes with us, in color, shape, or modes of use. A block of wood or stone contains, in the eye of the artistic workman, every possible grace of form and moulding; but a brick is a square, red, uninteresting fact, and the laying of them the most prosaic of all work. By common consent we expect no improvement in their use, but rather sigh for the good old times when work was honestly done and the size of the brick prescribed by law. We associate them with factories, boarding-houses, steam-chimneys, pavements, sewers,—whatever is practical, commonplace, and undignified. Yet there are charming, even delicate, effects possible with these unpromising rectangular blocks.

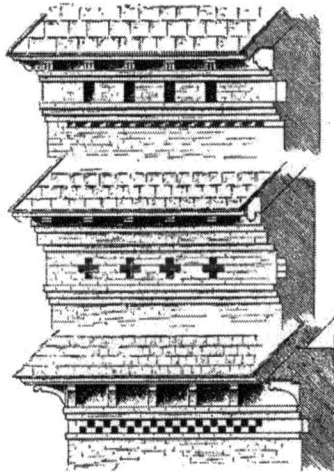

COTTAGE CORNICES

In your efforts to unite beauty and brickwork it will be well to begin modestly, merely aiming to avoid positive ugliness. Do not feel bound to enclose your house by four straight unbroken walls,—brick are no more difficult to build in irregular shape than anything else,—and do not, on any account, make square-topped openings, as the builders of the old-fashioned brick houses were wont to do. Doubtless you have read Mr. Ruskin's vigorous protest against this particular architectural sin; if you have not, by all means do so, only he proves too much, and would fain make us believe that our doors and windows must not only be crowned by arches, but they must be Gothic arches,—doctrine to be received with some grains of allowance. A pointed Gothic arch may be, often is, very beautiful; but, applying our test of utility, it is most obviously out of place, and therefore inartistic, where close economy, convenience, and abundance of light are required. For the sake of strength, if for no other reason, let the top of the openings be arched, but a low arch of one arc or two is often preferable to a high one. If, for economy's sake, you wish to make the top of the sash square, do so, curving the upper portion of the frame as a sort of centre on which the masonry may rest; but do not attempt this if the openings are wide, and in any case relieve the wood segment by ornamental cutting or some other device, otherwise you will have a weak and poverty-stricken effect. Or you may use a straight lintel of stone, taking care to build a conspicuous, relieving arch above it of stone or colored brick. You will get the idea from the sketches, and see that there is room for endless variety of expression and ornament without violating any of the first principles, which you will do if you try to cover a square-headed opening with a "straight arch" of brick, or leave a light, horizontal stone cap without a protecting arch above it.

SQUARE HEADS WITH BRICK CAPS

LETTER XII.

From John.

THE WEAKNESS AND
SHAM OF BRICKWORK.

My Dear Architect: You must have had a brick in your hat when you launched your last letter. I suppose there's no doubt that brick walls will stand thunder and lightning in the shape of Chicago fire and Boston gunpowder better than anything else. In fact, I've always had a notion that if there are any houses in a certain place where they don't need them to keep out the cold, they must be made of brick, Milton's gorgeous testimony to the contrary notwithstanding. But when you undertake to show up the softness and beauty of brickwork, you soar a little too high for me. If our masons would only make walls that are able to bear their own weight; not use more than half as much mortar as brick, and that made of sand instead of dirt; if they would build chimney-flues that will carry the smoke to the top of the building, instead of leaving it to ooze out around the window-frames a dozen feet away, as I once saw it in a costly building belonging to one of our ex-governors, and remember that a wooden joist running square across a chimney-flue is pretty sure to get up a bigger draught than most of us care for; if they wouldn't fill up the inside of the wall with bricks that it isn't safe to drop for fear they can never be picked up again; in short, if they'd do the work that can't be seen half as well as what is in plain sight, I'd never say a word about beauty, I wouldn't even ask for those elegant caps the masons are so fond of poking out over windows. You can find at least ten thousand such in Springfield. Some folks paint them, sprinkle sand into the paint, and then go on their wicked way rejoicing in the notion that they have told such a cunning lie as "no feller can find out."

Now and then the corner of a brick building is cobbled up into blocks and polished off in the same style. If these are some of the beauties of brickwork, I pray you have me excused. If you have anything better to offer, go ahead, I'm open to conviction; would rather be knocked down by an argument than a brickbat any time.

Mrs. John says she doesn't care a straw about bricks, and hopes you won't spend much time talking about them. She's bound to have a stone house, whether or no, and wants you to give us your notions about inside fixings, especially the kitchen. (Between you and me, she wouldn't have said a word about the kitchen, if I hadn't accused her of caring for nothing but bay-windows and folding-doors.) Her sister Jane has been over to see her, and they've had a host of projects to talk over; part of 'em I get hold of and part of 'em I don't. Jane isn't married, but she's got some capital notions about housekeeping. Great on having things nice and handy inside, especially for doing the work, but she don't care much for the outside looks. So she hopes you will get out of the brick-yard as soon as possible. Of course, I shall read what you have to say whether they do or not, but don't run wild on the subject.

Yours,
JOHN.

LETTER XIII.

From the Architect.

SKILL DIGNIFIES THE MOST HUMBLE MATERIAL.

Dear John: Please tell Mrs. John and Sister Jane that I am as anxious to get into the kitchen as they are to have me; and if I can succeed in giving suggestions that shall make the domestic work, on which our comfort and happiness so largely depend, easier and pleasanter,—restoring the wellnigh lost art of housekeeping to its native dignity,—it will be a grander achievement than designing the most beautiful exterior that ever adorned a landscape. I'm perfectly aware that the outside appearance of the house is to the interior comfort thereof as the body to the soul,—no comparison possible between the two. Still, they must possess their souls in patience and allow me to work according to my own plan. Moreover, they must not neglect a careful study of the brick question. A decided opinion is a good thing, provided it is grounded on the truth; otherwise it is a stumbling-block.

For yourself, I assure you my head is level; would that all brickwork were equally so. Beauty and bricks are not incompatible; but remember, there is one beauty of brick, another beauty of stone, and another beauty of wood. Do not confound them or expect that what pleases in one can be imitated in the other. As you were admonished, some time ago, "be honest; let brick stand for brick," then make the most of them. Your criticism on a very common form of "brick-dressing" is quite to the point. Aside from the stupid folly of painting them to imitate stone, not only these window-caps, but all horizontal belts having any considerable projection are essentially unfit for brickwork. The mortar is almost sure to fail at the upper side, giving the whole a look of premature decay, even if well done at first. A level course of long stone, running through a wall of small stones or brick, gives greater strength by binding the whole together. This has not always a good excuse for extending beyond the wall-face. But a projecting belt of brick adds nothing either in appearance or in reality. If horizontal lines are required to diminish the apparent height of the building or affect its proportions, make them of brick of different color from those of the main wall or laid in different position. Remember this; fanciful brick decorations are quite sure to look better on paper than when executed. As a rule, the more complex the design the greater the discount. Such work is apt to have an unsafe appearance, as though the whole was at the mercy of the bottom brick.

FRAGMENTS OF BRICKWORK

Your own sense of fitness must decide what shall be the general character of your house, whether light, open, airy, or sober, solid, and dignified. If the latter, let the strength of the walls be evident. Set the window-frames as far back from the wall-face as possible, in spite of any obstacles the builders may raise; make the arches above the openings massive, and the recessed portions of the cornice or any other ornamental work deep and narrow. There are not the same objections to a recess as to a projection; it is better protected, any imperfection is less apparent, and the desired effect of shadow is more complete. Much variety in color will not increase the appearance of strength, but the expression will be emphasized by pilasters and buttresses; also by the low segment arches and wide piers.

On the other hand, for a lighter effect, make the windows wider and crown them with semi-circles or pointed Gothic arches. Leave out the corners of the piers in building them up; introduce belts of brick laid in various positions and of different colors, if you can get them, as I trust you may. Indeed, this very season, a brickmaker has reported himself prepared to furnish black bricks and buff, red bricks and gray, all of good and regular standing. You may be sure I gave him my blessing, and invited him to press on. I do not know whether he will prove to be the coming man in this department, but whoever brings a greater variety of brick in form and color within reasonably easy reach will do a good work that shall surely have its reward; for brick houses we must have, ugly ones we won't have, and rich decorations of stone we cannot afford for common use. Meantime, if you can do no better, do not hesitate to use brick that have been treated to a bath of hot tar. They may look old-fashioned, by and by. No matter; an old fashion, if it is a good one, is more to be admired for its age than despised. It is only by reason of its falseness and inconvenience that it becomes absurd.

In the same category with colored bricks (indeed, they are a sort of spiritualized bricks) are the brilliant-hued encaustic tile that are finding their way hither across the Atlantic. Let us hope that the greatest country in the world will not long send three thousand miles for its building materials. A variety of forms and sizes of bricks we may easily have when we demand it in earnest. Beyond question there is room for almost unlimited exercise of fancy in this direction. We only need the taste to design appropriate shapes and to use them aright. Mr. Ruskin mentions certain brick mouldings as being among the richest in Italy. The matter of size relates rather to construction than ornament, but it is very important here. I think it will some time seem as unreasonable to make brick of but one size and pattern as it would now be to have all timber sawn of uniform dimensions.

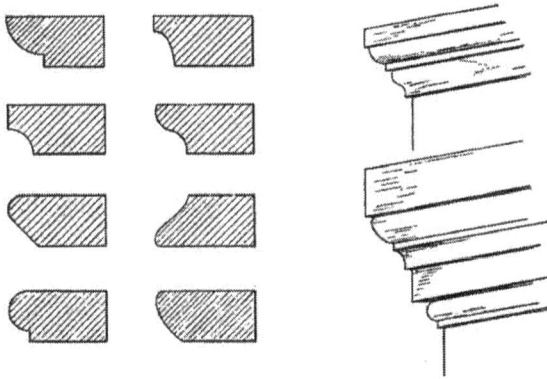

BRICKS THAT ARE NOT SQUARE

You are more liable to attempt too much in the way of decoration than too little. Don't make your house look as though it was intended for a brickmaker's show-case. You will find the simplest designs the best. I have seen a really good effect on the side of a large building from the mere holes left in the wall by the masons' stagings.

One thing more: Do not become possessed with the idea that a brick house must be a large or an expensive one. It may be small and cheap, but withal so cosey and domestic, so thoroughly tasteful and picturesque, that you will have an unquestioning faith in the possibility and the desirableness of love in a cottage, the moment you behold it. On the other hand, by making the best of your resources, it is possible to build a large, plain, square house, a perfect cube if you please, that shall not only be homelike in appearance, but truly impressive and elegant. How? I've been trying to illustrate and explain. By being honest; by despising and rejecting all fashions that have nothing but custom to recommend them; by using colored and moulded brick if you can use them well; by *not* laying the outside work in white mortar, and by exercising your common-sense and independence, both of which qualities I am sure you possess.

I must beg Mrs. John and Sister Jane (by the way, I'm flattered to know that a notable housekeeper finds anything promising in what I have thus far written you) not to give up the ship. One more broadside for the brick-yard, and we will pass on to loftier themes.

LETTER XIV.

From John.

EVERY MAN TO HIS TRADE.

My dear Architect: There is one point you might as well square up before you go any further. I understood that I was to build my house for myself to live in, not for my neighbors to look at. But I appeal to any white man, if you haven't had a deal more to say about the outside of the platter than the contents thereof. To be sure, it's what I might have expected. It's a way you architects have. You can no more help thinking how a house is going to look, than a woman can help hoping her first baby will be a beauty. I allow it would be a first-rate thing if we could have some streaks of originality, just a trifle more of variety, and a few glimpses of really good taste, along with the crumbs of comfort; and I'm willing to admit that your moves in that direction, as far as I can follow them, are all right. Still, it's a downright fact, that, unless a man is a great simpleton or a small Croesus, he is more anxious to make his house cosey and convenient, than he is to outshine his neighbors or beautify the landscape.

Sister Jane wants to know whether, in case one wishes to begin housekeeping on a small scale, it would be as easy to make additions to a brick house for future need, as to a wooden one. She doesn't ask on her own account, but for a friend of hers who is talking of building.

I expect you'll inquire pretty soon who's running these letters,—you or I; but if we don't sometimes show our ignorance by asking questions and making comments, how are you going to know what sort of information to shed?

Yours,
JOHN.

LETTER XV.

From the Architect.

THE COMING HOUSE WILL BE FAIR TO SEE AND MADE OF BRICK.

Dear John: Once for all, your questions and those of Sister Jane or any of her friends and relatives are always in order. The more the better. I will do my best to answer them, if not exactly by return mail, yet as soon as may be.

Other things being equal, a house built of brick may be as easily increased to suit a growing family as one built of wood. There is necessarily a loss attending any change in a finished building, yet it is often well to arrange one's plans with reference to future additions. Will it be in order for me to express to Sister Jane my approval of any young man who is willing to begin life on a small scale, undertaking no more than he can do honestly and well, yet with ambitious forethought providing for future increase? You seem to be slightly in error upon this point. I have not said you must build your house without any regard to the exterior, or intimated that it would even be right to do so. I only protest against building for the sake of the exterior,—against sacrificing thoroughness and interior comfort to outside display,—against using labor and material in such fashion that they are worse than thrown away, their whole result being false and tasteless,—against every kind of ostentation and humbug.

The truth is, we have all gone astray, literally, like sheep. We follow, for no earthly reason than because some one, not a whit wiser than we, happens to have rushed blindly in a certain direction.

"Of domestic architecture what need is there to speak! How small, how cramped, how poor, how miserable in its petty meanness, is our best! How beneath the mark of attack and the level of contempt, that which is common with us!"

Thus Mr. Ruskin on the domestic architecture of England. What would that merciless critic say, or rather what profundity of silence would he employ to express his opinion, of ours? It will be well for him and for us if he holds to his resolve never to visit America. This servile spirit of imitation, blind following of blind guides, is by no means confined to the outsides of our houses; it not only penetrates the interiors, but more or less influences all our affairs. Charge me with a professional interest if you will, I assure you no man can, in justice to himself or the community, build a house for his own use just like any other. He must attempt something better adapted to his needs and tastes than that can be which precisely suits some one else. If he can give no better reason for building as he builds, for furnishing as he furnishes, for living and thinking as he lives and thinks, than that another has done so before him, he may serve for the shadow of a man, but will never make the substance. Eastlake, another English authority, refers to continental cities and villages "the first glimpse of which is associated with a sense of eye-pleasure which is utterly absent in our provincial towns." And then, to drain the dregs of our humiliation, we are asked by his American editor to believe that, nevertheless, certain towns of the British Isles are miracles of picturesqueness "as compared with American towns, which have nothing but a succession of tame, monotonously ugly, and utterly uninteresting streets and squares to offer to the wearied eye." Yes, I am anxious about the outside of the house, but do not for a moment forget that it should always be subordinate to the weightier matters, the higher and holier uses of "home buildings."

62

PICTURESQUE AMERICA

Have I squared up your point? Let us return to the trowel.

The somewhat vexed question of mortar you shall answer according to your taste, so far as to choose between dark gray—"black" it is commonly called—and some shade of red, resembling the brick used. Between these two there seems to me to be one of those questions of taste, concerning which we are not permitted to dispute. With the dark mortar the joints will be visible, modifying the color of the wall, in some cases, perhaps, improving it; while the red will give a more uniform tint, on which not only colored brick or stone will appear to the best advantage, but the lines of the openings and other essential details are brought out in clearer relief. You would perhaps expect coloring the mortar the same shade as the brick to give precisely the effect of painting the entire wall. But it is not so. As in wood or stone, though in less degree, there is a kind of natural grain, even in the unnatural material, strengthened by oiling, but softer and richer than any painted surface. There seems to be no evidence that the mortar is injured by proper coloring-material,—mineral paints, or even lampblack, if you like it; I don't. Whether you like it or not, you are *not* to use *white* mortar for the outside work. Unless, indeed, you propose to build of pressed brick, in which case you will need it to show your neighbors how fearfully and wonderfully nice you are. If you are so devoted to worldly vanity as to build in that fashion in the country, I don't believe it will be possible for me to help you.

Chimneys deserve a chapter to themselves, they are so essential and so often abused. Let them start from the cellar-bottom and run straight and smooth to the very outlet. If you wish to be exceptionally careful and correct, use round pipe, cement or earthen, enclosed by brick. When it is so well known how often destructive fires are caused by defective flues, it is surprising that more care is not taken in building chimneys. They should be intrusted to none but workmen who are conscientious as well as skilful, otherwise every brick must be watched and every trowel full of mortar; for one defect ruins the whole, and five minutes after the fault is committed it can never be detected till revealed by the catastrophe.

If the spaces between the bricks were always filled with good mortar, it would be better not to plaster the inside of the flues, as the mortar is liable to cleave from the brick, and, hanging by one edge, form lodging-places for soot. As commonly built it is safer to plaster them within and without, especially without, for that can be inspected. The style of the visible part must depend upon the building. One thing lay up in the recesses of your lofty mind: A chimney is most useful and honorable, and you are on no account to be ashamed of it. Don't try to crowd it into some out-of-the-way corner, or lean it off to one side to clear a cupola,—better burn up the cupola,—or perch it daintily on a slender ridge like a brick marten-box; let it go up strong, straight, and solid, asserting its right to be, wherever it is needed, comely and dignified, and finished with an honest stone cap. Ruins are charming in the right place, but a tattered chimney-top on an otherwise well-preserved house is vastly more shabby than picturesque.

A common objection to brick houses is their redness; but there is no law against painting them, if their natural color is really inharmonious. Paint will improve the walls, will last longer on good brickwork than on wood, and there is no deception about it, unless you try to imitate stone. Still, it is not necessary, oil being just as good; and there is a sort of solid comfort in knowing that your house will look just as well fifty years hence as it does now, that it will mellow and ripen with age, and not need constant petting and nursing to preserve its tidiness.

The model house to which I alluded in beginning this subject will be, in brief, somewhat as follows: The outer walls will be vaulted, thoroughly non-conducting both of heat and of moisture. All the partitions will be of brick, precisely adapted in size to their use,—I am not sure but they will be hollow. The body of the floors will be of brick, supported, if need be, by iron ties or girders, all exactly fitted to the dimensions of the rooms, so that not a pound of material or an hour of labor shall be wasted on guess-work or in experiments. From turret to foundation-stone, the house will be a living, breathing, organic thing. If the weather prophet will declare what the average temperature of the winter is to be, we can tell to a hodful how much coal will maintain a summer heat throughout the establishment. You may be sure it will not be more than you now use in keeping two rooms uncomfortably hot and in baking the family pies. There will be no lathing, except occasionally on the ceilings; even this will not be necessary. You may make a holocaust of the contents of any room in the house, and, if the doors, finish, etc., happen to be of iron, as they may be, no one in the house will suspect your bonfire, until the heap of charcoal and ashes is found. Dampness and decay, unsavory odors and impure air, chilly bedrooms and cold floors, will be unknown. The ears in the walls will be stopped, there will be no settlement from shrinking timbers, no jelly-like trembling of the whole fabric when the master puts his foot down. Finally, the dear old house will be just as sound and just as lovely when the future John brings home his bride as when his grandsire built it. And it won't cost a cent more than the weak, unstable things we're raising by the thousand.

The coming house will surely be a brick one, but before it comes there will be plenty of work for the carpenters, and I shall not be at all surprised if you finally decide to build of wood.

LETTER XVI.

From Mrs. John.

DOMESTIC DISCIPLINE.

MR. ARCHITECT: Dear Sir,—Yesterday afternoon Sister Jane and I went out after May-flowers. We didn't find any, but on our way home met the schoolmaster, a friend of Jane's, who knew where they grew and offered himself as a guide. I was too tired to walk any farther, so they went off without me. Coming into the house, I was taken all aback by the sight of John lying on my best lounge, his muddy boots on his feet, his hat on the floor, and your last letter crumpled savagely in his hand. I was vexed, thankful, and—frightened.

I've taught the baby, who is only twenty-nine months old, to hang up his little cap, and not to climb into the chairs with his shoes on, but I can't make a model husband of John. He is as good as gold, but will leave his hat on the floor, his coat on the nearest chair, and never keeps himself or any of his things in order in the house. He says it's born with him; comes from a long line of ancestors (he's been reading Darwin lately) who lived in houses without any cupboards or drawers or closets, and he could no more put away his hat and coat when he comes in than a blue-jay could build a hang-bird's nest. Yes; I was vexed, but thankful, too, that Jane was out of sight. Of all people in the world; she has the least mercy for anything like domestic untidiness. I only hope she will some time have a house and a husband of her own; if one doesn't shine and the other shake, her practice will fall a long way behind her preaching. Let me warn you now, not to attempt making any plans for her. It will be worry and vexation of spirit from first to last. Every knot will be examined, every shingle ironed flat before it is laid, every nail counted and driven by rule. When I tell her it would wear me out, body and mind, to feel obliged to keep things always in order, she gravely reminds me that Mrs. Keep-clean lived ten years longer than Mrs. Clean-up, besides having an easier time, a tidy house, and an enviable reputation all her life. Yes; I was thankful she had gone philandering off after May-flowers, and hoped she would stay till I had had time to brush up the room and get John into presentable shape. But as soon as I went to rouse him I was thoroughly frightened. His face was flushed, his hair was ruffled, and he looked up in such a dazed kind of way, I really thought he was going to have something dreadful. He held out your letter and told me to read the last sentence, which I did. Even then I didn't understand what was the trouble until he went on to say that your final charge was too much for him. He was totally discouraged. You began, he said, by urging him to build a stone house, which neither of us liked, though we finally came around to it,—even went so far as to commence hauling stones. All at once you went into ecstasies over brickwork, and argued for it as though our hope of salvation lay in our living in a brick house. Now, as he was beginning to feel that he must change his mind again (he would almost as soon change his head) and cultivate an admiration for brickwork, you must needs switch off upon another track and coolly advise him to build of wood! He declared he was further from a new house to-day than three months ago. At that rate we should live in the old one till it tumbled down over our heads, which I don't propose to do.

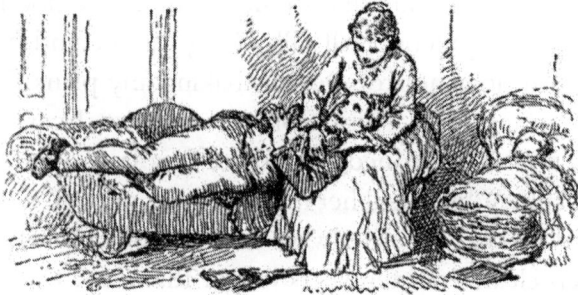

A WISE GENERAL

The baby was asleep, so I sat down on the lounge, took John's head in my lap, and tried to explain what you meant. I told him I had heard enough about brick, and didn't care what you said about wood. We should hold to our original plan and have a stone house; but you didn't know where it was to be, and wished us to be thoroughly posted, then use our common-sense and decide for ourselves what it should be. In some places it would be most absurd to build of wood; in others equally so to build of anything else. The matter of cost, too, might affect our choice, and that you knew nothing about.

In my efforts to restore his equanimity, I had forgotten my broom and dust-pan, lying in the middle of the floor; forgotten John's big boots, not only on the lounge, but directly on one of Jane's most exquisite tidies; forgotten—actually forgotten—the baby, and was treating my disturbed husband in genuine ante-matrimonial style, when, of all things to happen at this very crisis, in marched Sister Jane and her cavalier! Simultaneously the baby awoke with a resounding scream.

Now there are three things that my notable sister holds in especial abhorrence,—untidy housekeeping, sentimental demonstrations between married people, and crying babies; and here they all were in an avalanche, overwhelming, not only herself, but a most prepossessing young man, who, for all I knew, was viewing me with a critic's eye, as a possible sister-in-law, and wondering how far certain traits are universal in families.

You will think I stand in great awe of Sister Jane; and so I do, for though she is two years younger than I, unmarried, and, candidly, not a bit wiser, she is one of those oracular persons who, unlike Mr. Toots, not only fancy that what they say and do is of the utmost consequence, but contrive to make other people think so, too.

It is one of my husband's notions that nothing in the house is too good to be used every day by those he loves best, meaning baby and I. So I have no parlor—no best room always ready for exhibition—into which I could send them, but my inspiration came just at the right moment.

"Don't, Jane, don't, for pity's sake, bring all that rubbish into the sitting-room!" She had her hands full of moss and flowers. "Please take it out on the piazza. John will carry you some chairs." And Jane was positively too much astonished to say a single word, but turned and walked out the way she came in, driving her dutiful escort before her.

Fortunately, our piazza is eight or nine feet wide. I wouldn't have one less than that. So John took out the chairs, and was properly presented to the young gentleman.

Half an hour later, when order once more prevailed, I went out to find Jane finishing a lovely moss basket, and the gentlemen amiably building air-castles. John had been reading your last letter aloud, omitting your reply to Jane's question, and was advocating brick in a most edifying fashion. As I sat down, the young man inquired very seriously if there would be any difficulty in making additions to a brick house, in case one wished to begin in a small way. John gave one of his queer looks, and guessed not; I, for a wonder, kept still; and Jane blushed brilliantly, remembering that she had already asked the same question on her friend's account.

I am, truly, anxious about the kitchen and closets, whatever nonsense my husband may write, but should be sorry to have the house look just like any other, and, of course, wish to have it look well. Why may not our stone house be built in the manner of your model brick one, at least basement and first story, thoroughly warmed and ventilated, brick partitions, fire-proof, and so on,—that is, if we can afford it? And that brings me to the question that I intended to ask in the beginning, Are these suggestions intended to apply to common kind of buildings or only to those that are usually described as "first class"? Architectural rules and the principles of good taste are not thought to concern those who, in building, know no law but necessity,—with whom the problem is to get the greatest amount of use for the least possible outlay.

John is industrious and serene, this morning. He thinks my letter isn't very practical, and hopes you won't forget that the subject in hand is house-building, not family history.

Yours truly,
MRS. JOHN.

LETTER XVII.

From the Architect.

GOOD TASTE IS NOT A FOE BUT A FRIEND TO ECONOMY.

MRS. JOHN: Dear Madam,—For your wise and tender treatment of John you have my heartiest thanks and admiration. It is not strictly an architectural suggestion, but could you not found a sort of training-school for wives who have not learned to manage their refractory husbands? I'm sure you would have plenty of pupils.

Your query as to applying these hints I am glad to answer. Instead of preventing its indulgence, close economy demands the exercise of the most refined taste. The very houses that must pay strict regard to the first principles of art are those upon which not one dollar can be wasted. But these fundamental rules are identical, whether the building costs five hundred dollars or fifty thousand. When the newspapers describe "first-class" houses, those above a certain size or cost are meant. Let us henceforth have a truer standard, placing only those in the front rank whose design and construction are throughout in wise accord with the material of which they are built and the uses for which they are intended.

Notwithstanding your want of interest in the wood question, I must give your husband one chapter on that subject, and promise him it shall be thoroughly practical, free from all romance and family allusions.

LETTER XVIII.

From John.

OUR PICTURESQUE ANCESTORS.

MY DEAR ARCHITECT: I've no doubt it would be vastly agreeable to you to have Mrs. John keep up this end of the correspondence. Very gratifying, too, to another party,—the paper-makers. It would be a big thing for them. But I don't want to hire a housekeeper, even in so good a cause, not till I have a house.

In spite of Mrs. John's devotion to her first love (I mean the stone walls), it is, as you say, quite possible that our family mansion will be wood; and Barkis is willin' to hear what you have to say about it.

One topic in your reply to my wife's historical report I hope you will work up more fully. Just explain, if you can, why the cheap buildings we have nowadays are so much less satisfactory to look at than those built fifty or a hundred years ago. Do you suppose the bravest artist that ever swung a brush would dare put an ordinary two-story house of modern style on the front seat in a New England landscape? It would ruin his reputation if he did,—even without the French roof. Can you tell why? There's no such objection to the homesteads of a generation or two ago. Don't tell me age is venerable, and moralize about the sacred associations and old-time memories that lend a halo of poetry and romance and what-'s-his-name to these relics of the past. That's all very well in its place, but if our grandchildren can discover anything artistic or even picturesque in our common houses of to-day, they'll be a progeny of enormous imaginations,—regular Don Quixotes; windmills will be nothing to them.

Yours,
JOHN.

LETTER XIX.

From the Architect.

THE USE AND THE ABUSE OF WOOD.

DEAR JOHN: One reason, among many, why the old-time houses are more grateful to the eye than those of similar cost but modern style, is that they were built of wood honestly and legitimately used, when wood was on all accounts the most suitable material for building. It is so still, and will be for a long time in many places, for its economy and convenience. Given a fair chance, it may be made very durable, and is even rendered practically fire-proof without great cost, by kyanizing and various other methods that are adopted for the same purpose. You will find one mode described in the June number of Harper's Magazine for 1870. Wood is effective, too, in appearance, when rightly used, which, more's the pity, does not often happen; for of all the materials that minister to human comfort and needs, this seems to me the most abused. Iron, like the old-time saints, betrays not its solid worth till it has been tried by fire,—is all the better for being hammered and beaten; stone is as much improved as an unruly boy by a good dressing; while bricks, like ghosts, come forth from their purgatory for the express purpose of being laid. All of these, by appropriate treatment, are invested with graces and glories that by nature they never owned. But a tree, graceful, noble, and grand beyond all human imitation, is ignominiously hewn down, every natural beauty disguised or annihilated, and its helpless form compelled to assume most uncouth shapes and grimmest colors.

THE GROVES WERE GOD'S FIRST TEMPLES

Of late our injustice is greater and more disastrous; for we are destroying the very sources of supply without providing for the future, using wood in large quantities where other materials would be better and cheaper. Yet we think ourselves very economical. Once it was common to enclose wood buildings of all grades by walls at least ten or twelve inches thick, sometimes much more, and solid at that. They were called log-houses. Now it is the fashion to use two by four inch studs standing in rows at such distances that the whole substance of the frame in a single sheet would be about half an inch thick. These are suggestively called balloon frames. The former would be huge and inconvenient, the latter are often fair and frail. That the frame of the outer wall of a wooden building should be mainly vertical is evident, the outer studs, if possible, extending from the sill to the plates, and as many of the inner ones as may be reaching through both stories, especially those by the staircase, where the shrinking of the second-floor timbers will reveal ugly cracks and crooks. That the greatest strength and economy of material are secured by sawing logs into thin, wide scantling is also beyond question, but don't try to save too closely on a bill of timber. A thousand feet added to the width of the studs and the depth of the joist will make the difference between a stiff, unterrified frame, and a weak, trembling one. Neither be sparing of the number of these light sticks. Sixteen inches between centres is far enough for studs or joists; twelve is better, though particulars will depend on circumstances. We have no use for the old-fashioned huge square posts, horizontal girts, and braces midway the walls of a two-story building, having found that studs two inches by five will carry all that is required of them as well as if ten times as large. Let us generously give the light frame the stanch support of a sound, well-matched, and bountifully nailed covering of inch boards. There's great virtue in tenpenny nails. Let the building be well peppered with them. Even after boarding, your walls will have less than two inches of solid wood. If you wish to make an example of yourself, lay this boarding diagonally; and, to cap the climax of scientific thoroughness, having given it a good nailing and a layer of sheathing-felt, cover the whole with another wooden garment of the same style as the first, and crossing it at right angles. All of this before the final overcoat of clapboards, or whatever it may be. A house built in this way would laugh at earthquakes and tornadoes. It couldn't fall down, but would blow over and roll down hill without doing any damage except disarranging the furniture, and, possibly, shaking off the chimney-tops! It would hardly need any studs except as furrings for lath and plastering, and would be very warm. You know my mind about floors. If you can't afford joists stiff enough to hold you without jarring, even when you chance to cut a caper with the baby, defer building till you are a little richer. Floors need the well-nailed linings, too, especially those of the upper stories, almost as much as the outer walls, and should be deafened with mortar if you can stand the cost; if not, with felt. The upper floors we will talk over by and by. Some people have a fancy for filling in between studs with soft brick, but I don't believe in it. It is seldom well done, it injures the frame, and costs more than back plastering, without being much if any better. Rather build a brick house outright. It is well, however, to lay a course or two of brick in mortar against each floor, filling the space between the inner base board and the outer covering entirely full and solid, leaving never the faintest hint of the beginning of a chance for mice. Then when you hear the dear little creatures galloping over the ceiling, driving hickory-nuts before them and making noise enough for a whole battalion of wharf rats, there will be a melancholy satisfaction in knowing that you did your best to keep them out, and these brick courses will make the house warmer by preventing currents of air.

Here is one advantage in wood not easily obtained in brick or stone,— the overhanging of the whole, or a part of the second story, which may be made picturesque in effect and will add much to the charm of the interior. It may be simply an oriel window swinging forward to catch the sun or a distant view, an entire gable pushing the guest-chamber hospitably forth, or the whole upper story may extend beyond the lower walls, giving large chambers, abundant closets, and cosey window-seats. Of course, such projections must be well sustained. Let their support be apparent, in the shape of massive brackets or the actual timbers of the house.

Speaking of brackets, if we could learn to think of them, wherever they occur, simply as braces, we might have better success in their treatment. Our abominable achievements in this line spring from an attempt to hide the use of the thing in its abstract beauty. The straight three by four inch braces found under any barn-shed roof are positively more agreeable to look at than the majority of the distorted, turned, and becarved blocks of strange device that hang in gorgeous array upon thousands of "ornamental" houses. Besides these there are a host of pet performances of builders and would-be architects that deserve only to be abolished and exterminated; put up, as they are, with an enormous waste of pine and painful toil of the flesh, to become a lasting weariness to the spirit. Far more satisfying and truly ornamental is it, to let the essential structure of the building be its own interpreter. Very much can be done by a skilful arrangement of the outer covering alone. Don't try to clothe the house with a smooth coat of boards laid horizontally with no visible joints or corner finish. Such a covering is costly, defective, and contrary to first principles. Clapboards are good. Hardly anything is better, but don't feel restricted to one mode. I send you some sketches suggesting what may be done in this department by a careful design in the use of wide boards and narrow boards, clapboards and battens; boards horizontal, vertical, and cornerwise,—any and all are legitimate, and it may be well to use them all on one building.

OUTER FINISH OF WOOD

Many points relating to the use of wood and appertaining equally to buildings whose walls are of brick or stone, we may find farther on. In closing, let me adjure you by all your hope of a comfortable, safe, and satisfying house,—by all the common-sense in your possession and all the capital at your command,—resolve that you will never—no, never—build your house of unseasoned timber.

LETTER XX.

From John.

A SURRENDER AND CHANGE OF BASE.

MY DEAR ARCHITECT: It was very well for Noah and the other antediluvians, who had any little building to do, to wait for their timber to season. When a man has a thousand years or so to live, he can afford to take things easy. It's different in this great and glorious nineteenth century, when the chief aim is to make the shortest time on record. You know our Western farmers have a brisk way of going out into their thousand-acre wheatfields before breakfast, reaping, threshing, and grinding the grain, which their thrifty wives make into biscuit for the morning meal; and you've heard of the young man who caught a sheep in the morning, sheared it, carded, spun, and wove the wool, cut the cloth and made the coat to wear at his own wedding in the evening. Young America don't understand why a pine or an oak tree can't be put over the course, like a sheep or an acre of grain. Besides, you talk like an old fogy. When a man says he has decided to build a house, he means he is ready to begin,—right off; and if our lumber-dealers won't keep dry stuff (which of course they won't unless obliged to), then he must use green.

I'm surprised you don't admire the fanciful brackets and other wooden straddle-bugs people are so fond of decorating their houses with. By the way, if these brackets are purely ornamental, there ought not to be two alike, any more than you'd have two busts or two pictures alike in one room. Suppose you collect an assortment of the rich and rarest specimens, and hang them, like Lord Dundreary's shirts, "all in a wo," on somebody's villa. Wouldn't they be lovely? I'd like to pursue the subject, but have other fish to fry.

Mrs. John is right, as usual; our house will be a stone one, and will not be built until next year. Meantime, the timber will have a chance to season, and we shall have time to study up our plan and sort of get the hang of it.

Now I want you to transfer your interest to another case. Who should drop down upon us, last week, but our old friend Fred? Been out West for the last dozen years or more; enterprising and prosperous, you'll be glad to hear. Come home to stay, bringing a wife who is sure to make Mrs. John jealous, a triplet of boys (the oldest half as big as his dad), and plenty of stamps. He has bought the Captain Adams place, and is going to move off the old gambrel-roofed house (has a dozen or two men at work already) and build a brick one in place of it. I've given him the benefit of your advice in my behalf, and now he invites me, in Western fashion, to stand aside and give him a chance,—which I'm very willing to do, for he's a tiptop fellow and so is Mrs. Fred. Eastern people Westernized,—if you can find a better sort of neighbors I'd like an introduction!

Yours,
JOHN.

LETTER XXI.

From the Architect.

HOSPITALITY AND SUNLIGHT.

DEAR JOHN: Our old friend shall not be neglected. He has only to present his case and make known his wishes. Meantime, in arranging your own plans, be generous if you can; not lavish or extravagant in expenditure, but generous in feeling and expression. Let your doors and windows be wide, and your roof be high. A wide door is far more convenient than a narrow one, usually much better in appearance; and for the windows,—when shall we learn the unspeakable worth of the bountiful light of heaven? Does Mrs. John complain that the sunlight will fade her carpets? Let them fade, and know of a truth that all the colors of all the carpets of all the looms that ever throbbed are not worth to the civilized mortals who tread the dust-containing fabrics one single hour of unobstructed sunshine. Is it that our deeds are evil, that we seem to love darkness rather than light; or is it through our ignorant exclusion of this glorious gift, "offspring of heaven first born," that we are left to wander in so many darksome ways? Be generous, did I say? rather try to be just to yourself. Practically, the larger opening is scarcely more expensive than the small one. The work of construction is no greater, and the material for the door or window costs but little more than the thicker wall of wood, brick, or stone.

THE OLD HOUSE AT HOME

I remember an old farm-house on the side of one of our rocky New England hills, a type of a fashion almost extinct, broad and brooding, low in the walls, small windows and far between, high roof, wide gables, pierced by windows of various sizes, and queerly located, as if the huge garret were inhabited by a mixed company of dwarfs and giants, each with his own particular window suited to his height; in the centre a massive chimney like the base of a tower, out of which the smoke rolled in lazy curves. At the east side of the house, under the narrow eaves, and opening, I think, into the long kitchen, was one huge window, as high as the others, and as wide as it was high. How it found a place there I never knew, but nothing could be more benign in effect than its generous breadth. The panes were small and green and warped, after the manner of glass known to former times; but through it the sun poured a flood of warm light every morning, and on winter evenings the glow of the firelight within made a grand illumination far across the snowy hillsides; yet I don't think the old window was ever truly appreciated. The others seemed to despise it, and try to keep at a distance in their narrowness and regularity. The little square loopholes in the gables lifted their diminutive eyebrows in contempt; even the green door looked blank and scowling, as though at a possible rival. I fancy the housekeeper fretted at the larger curtain covering this wide, unwinking eye, and the extra labor required on cleaning-days. But this one great square window was the sole redeeming feature beneath the roof of the ancient farm-house. Beneath the roof, I say. The roof itself was, and is, and ever shall be the great charm of those antiquated houses,—not of the old alone, but if any new house shall ever rise, if you succeed in building your own so that it shall seem to be the abiding-place of the incarnate genius of domestic happiness, the roof of your earthly paradise will be bold and high. Pierced by windows it may be, and broken by gables, but steep enough to shed rain and snow, and high enough to be plainly visible to the coming guest, promising safety and welcome beneath its tranquil shade. Practically, the steep roof is better than any other, because a flat one cannot be as permanently covered with any known material at so little cost, the multitudes of cheap and durable patent roofings to the contrary notwithstanding. By steep roofs I mean any that have sufficient pitch to allow the use of slate or shingle. Such need not be intricate or difficult of construction to look well, but must be honest and useful. They can be neither unless visible, and here we see the holy alliance of use and beauty; for the character and expression of a building depend almost wholly upon the roof. You will lose, too, under the flat roof, the roomy garret of the old high-roofed houses. These have for me a wonderful fascination. Whether the rain upon the shingles, the mingled fragrance of seeds and drying herbs, the surprising bigness of the chimney, the mysteries hidden in the worm-eaten chests, the almost saintly charm of the long-unused spinning-wheels, crumbling mementos of the patient industry of former generations, or the shine of the stars through the chinks in the shrunken boards, the old garret and all its associations are among the "long, long thoughts." I sometimes doubt whether the modern conveniences we are so fond of proclaiming are really an equivalent to the rising generation for this happiest of playrooms, this storehouse of heirlooms, this silent but potent tie, that binds us to the life, the labor, and the love of the past.

FORTY-TWO FEET SQUARE

Let there be light, too, in this upper story. Spinning spiders and stinging wasps are not half so terrible to the children who will make a half-way paradise of the garret as the darkness that is covered by an unlighted roof.

If you have been living in cottage-chambers,—rooms in which a full-sized man can hardly stand erect in the centre, and a well-grown baby scarcely creep at the sides, unventilated, heated beyond endurance during the hot summer days, and retaining their heat through the long, wakeful nights,—rooms in which the furniture must stand at various distances from the walls as if marshalled for the house-cleaning battle, but in which even the making of beds is a work of supreme difficulty,—if you've been living in such rooms as these, I don't wonder, whatever architects or other men may say, that Mrs. John objects, and insists on good, square chambers. But good, square chambers no more require flat roofs than good, square common-sense requires a flat head. I don't believe you will contrive a house, of whatever form or size, that may not be covered more cheaply, more securely, and more tastefully by a steep roof than by a flat one. Of course, I'm supposing your house to be isolated. Buildings in crowded streets or in blocks require, on all accounts, entirely different treatment. By all means, then, have wide doors, generous windows, and high roofs; and if you must build with strict economy you may be morally certain that your house, though not perhaps as altogether lovely as you might wish, will still be cheerful and homelike.

Allow me to add, that, while faithfully striving to build a house that shall be honest and cheerful, you will surely find yourself growing in the same direction.

LETTER XXII.

From Fred.

UNPROFESSIONAL SAGACITY.

DEAR ARCHITECT: Our mutual friend John recommends me to ask your advice in regard to plans for my new house. Possibly you may help me, although the floor plans sent herewith are about right; rooms enough and of the right size, the principal ones adapted to the usual widths of carpeting. I am willing to expend something for the outside appearance,—in fact, intend to have the best looking house in town,— but think it would be foolish to build more rooms or larger than I want, much more so to dispense with needed room in order to get a certain proportion of parts. I merely mention this because, with all due respect, I am doubtless the best judge of my own wants, and don't care to have the dimensions of the building changed. The relative location of the different apartments is also satisfactory, except perhaps some slight deficiencies in the rear portion, which I left incomplete for want of time. As to exterior, would like a French roof and tower, with fashionable style of finish throughout.

Shall commence laying foundation next week, and you will please consider yourself invited to eat turkey with us in the new house next Thanksgiving.

Truly,
FRED.

LETTER XXIII.

From the Architect.

STAIRWAYS AND OUTLOOKS.

Dear Fred: Your plans are before me, also your letter; also the proverbs of Solomon, from which I read, in order to fortify myself for the work before me, sundry suggestions concerning the duty of faithful friends,— the undaunted, disagreeable sort who cry aloud and spare not. It's quite right for you to try to show what you would like, quite true that you ought to know your own needs and tastes better than any one else, and though I cannot agree with you, I'm glad you have a mind of your own; those who have not are of all men most miserable to deal with, most difficult to suit. Indeed, when a man feels clearly a lack in his own home-life which nothing but a new house will supply, he is sure to have some decided notions as to what that house shall be. But when you assure me in good set terms that this plan is your beau-ideal, I must ask, also with profound respect, if you know what you are talking about. Put in your foundation, by all means, but remember how much easier it is to change a few lines on paper than to remove a stone wall. It is not a pleasant job to cut a door into a finished and furnished room, or even to change the hanging of it. This house, if I understand aright, you intend for a permanent home. How immeasurably better to spend six months, if need be, in perfecting the plans, than by and by to be tormented with defects that can only be removed by great expense and trouble! It's a grand thing to go ahead, provided you are right; the more "go," the worse, if you happen to be on the wrong track. Candidly, your plan hardly deserves to be called a beginning. The arrangement of the rear part, which you chiefly omit, is, in fact, the most difficult and important of the whole. But I've promised Sister Jane a chapter on kitchens, of which, when the time comes, you can have the benefit. Meanwhile, complete the unfinished part of your plan,—it only requires you to spend a few brief moments,—and I will venture some suggestions on this which lies before me.

The front stairs as laid down would reach just half-way to the second floor,—a peculiarity of amateur sketches so universal that we will say nothing more about it. But what principle of good taste or hospitality requires you to blockade the main entrance to your house with this same staircase? Do you send all your visitors, of whatever name or nation, direct to the upper regions the moment they enter? Why, then, make the northwest passage thither the most conspicuous route from the door? Do you intend to restrict the family to the back stairs, which by your showing are, like the famous *descensus Averno*, wonderfully easy to go down, but mighty hard to get up again? Yet you place these front stairs at the very farthest remove from the rooms most constantly used in both stories. Perhaps you propose to announce "apartments to let" on the second and third floors. No? What reason, then, for imitating hotels, lodging-houses, double-barrelled tenements, and other public and semi-public buildings from which a short cut to the street is essential? Don't tell me you wish them to be ornamental as well as useful. I know that; but remember the stairs are built for the house, not the house for the stairs. You had better lose them wholly as an ornamental feature, than destroy the charm of what should be the most prepossessing portion of the interior. Moreover, they can have no pleasure-giving beauty if manifestly out of place,—a safe rule for general application. Build them where they will be most useful, that is, as near the centre of the house as possible; make them grand and gorgeous as the steps to an Oriental palace,—so broad and easy of ascent that the upward and onward way will be as tempting as were the Alps to Mr. Longfellow's aspiring youth. But keep them away from the front door,—out of the principal hall, which should be open, airy, and free, suggesting something besides an everlasting getting up stairs. If the staircase hall cannot be arranged at right angles to the main hall, an arch or ornamental screen may be introduced, partially separating the two and giving character to both.

Have you been living in a city of late? It must be, else why so complacent with a narrow hall, steep, obtrusive stairs, and, O, why, tell me why, do you not fix the location of your windows with some regard to views, not only out of the house but through it. I remember one country dwelling built by a retired civilian in the inevitable city style; windows at the end giving a narrow view of the road in front, while the entire side walls were absolutely blank and bare, never so much as a knot-hole through which the occupants could get a glimpse of the field and forest that stretched broadly away at either side. I've no doubt the owner hung oil-paintings on his parlor walls, and thought them more lovely than all out-doors,— especially when he remembered their cost. The old Roman who declared his soldiers made a bigger racket with their arms than Jupiter with his thunderbolts, was modest beyond comparison with such a man. Your arrangement is not quite so bad as that of the aforesaid civilian, but, like hosts of others, you fail to make the most of your opportunities. Suppose you were able to secure for a small sum a landscape painted by one of the masters and esteemed of great value. You would think it folly to let the chance pass unimproved. By simply cutting a hole in the wall you may have a picture infinitely grander than human artist ever painted; grander in its teaching, in its actual beauty, its variety, and its permanency; grander in everything except its market value. I am not sure but your children's children will find some one window in the old homestead that commands a view of the everlasting hills, an heirloom even of greater pecuniary value than the rarest work of art. Do not forget, either, the views *through* the house. If your windows can be placed so that throwing open the doors from room to room or across the hall will reveal a charming prospect in opposite directions, there's a sense of being in the midst of an all-surrounding beauty, hardly possible when you seem to look upon it from one side only. You have surely been abiding in a city. The interior of your house is all that concerns you or your family. The outside—French roof and fashionable finish, forsooth!—is for the public to admire. They are not to have any intimation what sort of a home is sheltered by your monstrous Mansard; and it never occurs to you that there can be anything out of doors worth building your house to see.

LOOK OUT, NOT IN

Here is another unhappy result of evil examples,—the sliding-doors between the two parlors, as you call them,—an arrangement convenient enough, sometimes indispensable in houses built on crowded streets, houses that only breathe the dusty air and catch the struggling sunbeams at their narrow and remote extremities,—air and sunlight at nobody knows how many hundred dollars the front foot. They are worse than useless in such a house as yours.

I say your plan is scarcely a beginning; the same of this letter. But it's enough for once.

LETTER XXIV.

From Fred.

IN A MULTITUDE OF COUNSELLORS IS SAFETY.

MY DEAR ARCHITECT: Your criticisms are not wholly without reason. I can only plead haste and inexperience.

Have been studying arrangement of rear part, and seem to get farther and farther from a satisfactory result. The kitchen and dining-room must be convenient to each other, but not adjacent; the pantries and larder easy to get at; back stairs accessible from all parts of the house, and side entrance worked in somehow; washbowl and water-closet not far off, but out of sight, and the whole department quite isolated from front hall. My wife can't think of pantry and store-rooms at the south side, nor do we want kitchen or outer door at the north. John's sister-in-law, Miss Jane, who appears to have some sensible notions, thinks a kitchen should always have windows on opposite sides for light and ventilation. John says I should have a kitchen large enough for wash-trays and a set kettle, but one of my neighbors, who has just built a house, advises a laundry in the cellar. Altogether it 's a troublesome problem, and, frankly, I give it up.

Do you really expect us to dispense with sliding-doors between the parlors? I'm sure that won't pass. We would almost as soon give up the bay-windows,—everybody has them nowadays.

Truly,
Fred.

LETTER XXV.

From the Architect.

DOORS AND SLIDING-DOORS, WINDOWS AND BAY-WINDOWS.

DEAR FRED: "Everybody has them!" What a monstrous load of iniquity and nonsense that scape-goat has to carry! Everybody wears tight boots and bustles and chignons and stove-pipe hats. Everybody smokes and brags, and cheats in trade, not to mention a host of other abominations that can give only this excuse for their being: they are common to a few millions of people who have not learned to declare a reason for the faith that is in them or the works that grow out of them.

Let us take time to consider this sliding-door question,—folding-doors they used to be, and, truly, I'm not sure that the rollers are any improvement on the hinges,—there is something dreadfully barny about sliding-doors. Why do you want either? You have one room which you call the parlor, supposed to be the best in the house, as to its location, its finish, its furniture, and its use. Three of its walls are handsomely frescoed, curtained, and decorated with pictures or other ornaments; the fourth is one huge barricade of panel-work. When the two parts are closed you have a constant fancy of rheumatic currents stealing through the cracks, and an ever-present fear lest they should suddenly fly open with "impetuous recoil, grating harsh thunder" on their wheels, and not exactly letting Satan in, but everything in the room fall out; an idle fear, for they can only be shoved asunder by dint of much pushing and pulling, especially if they are warped by having one side exposed to more heat than the other, as usually happens. Being at last opened by hook or crook, another room is revealed, commonly smaller, more shabby in appearance, a sort of poor-relation attachment, spoiling the completeness and artistic unity of the larger one. By care you may avoid something of this; if you follow the fashion, you will have the most of it. When the two rooms are twins, alike in every respect, they are really one large room, fitted up, for economical reasons, with a movable screen in the centre, by means of which you may warm (excepting rheumatic currents as above) and use one half at a time. But call things by their right names. Don't talk grandly about your two parlors when you mean two halves of one. Have wide doors, by all means, not only between rooms but into main hall,—four, six, or eight feet, if the rooms are so wide and high that they shall not be disproportionately large. Then, if you must have the whole broadside of sliding or folding doors, let the two rooms thus connected be of different styles but equal richness,—different, that they shall not seem one room cut in two,—peers, that one shall not shame and cheapen the other.

Doors are a great bother, at best. I wish they could be abolished. They are always slamming, punching holes in the plastering with their knobs, creaking on their hinges, bruising the piano, pinching babies' fingers, and making old folks see stars when they get up in the night to look for burglars. Heavy curtains are infinitely more graceful, equally warm, and not half so stubbornly unmanageable. Then think of entering a room. By her steps the goddess is revealed; but who can walk like a goddess while forcing an entrance between two sliding-doors, maybe wedging fast half-way through? How different from passing in quiet dignity beneath the rich folds of overhanging drapery! But I suppose we must leave all that to the Orientals, at present.

"You would almost as soon give up the bay-windows!" Well, you might e'en do worse than that. Now let your indignation boil. Bay-windows are very charming things sometimes; sometimes they are nuisances. Some have been so appropriate and altogether lovely that any pepper box contrivance thrusting itself out from the main walls and looking three ways for Sunday is supposed to be a bower of beauty, a perfect pharos of observation, an abundant recompense for unmitigated ugliness and inconvenience in the rest of the building. Truly, a well-ordered bay-window will often change a gloomy, graceless room into a cheerful and artistic one, but large, simple windows are sometimes rather to be chosen than too much bay. In many, perhaps the majority, of cases, it is wiser to extend the whole wall of the room in the form of a half-hexagon or three sides of an octagon, costing no more, and repaying the cost far more abundantly.

While on the subject let us finish it. If you indulge in a regular bay-window, make it large enough to be of real use; don't feel constrained to build it with more than fifteen sides; remember that two stories will not cost twice as much as one, while the second is pretty certain to be the pleasanter; don't carry the ceiling of the main room level and unbroken into the bay, or, because a certain one you may have seen looks well in its place, resolve to have another just like it, regardless of its surroundings. I sometimes fancy there must be a factory where bay-windows are made for the wholesale trade, all of one style, strictly orthodox, five-sided, bracketed, blinded, painted with striped paint, and ready to barnacle on wherever required. In the stereotyped pattern the blinds are apt to be troublesome. If outside, they clash against each other and refuse to be fastened open; while inside they are a mighty maze of folds, flaps, brass buts, and rolling slats. In the first case, wide piers between the sash are necessary; in the second, boxings for the blinds. Both require ample room, which, fortunately, you have. Sixthly, and in conclusion, there is no one feature which may be more charming, combining so much of comfort and beauty, as windows of this class, from the simple opening, pushed forward a few inches beyond the wall face, to the broad extension of the entire room; but there be bays and bays.

Speaking of blinds,—what shall be done with the other windows? You will protest against concealing your elegant, single panes of plate-glass by outside blinds,—it won't answer to hide your light under a bushel in that way,—and yet while there is no complete finish without well-arranged inside shutters, they alone are sadly inefficient in rooms with a southern exposure, where light and air are needed. They may be fitted with boxings, into which they are folded, or arranged to slide into the wall. I like the old-fashioned boxing, window-seat and all, also the ancient close-panelled shutters. True they make a room pitch-dark when closed, and it is doubtless wisest to have some of their central folds made with movable slats, but they give a charming sense of security and seclusion when the wintry blasts roar around our castle. On the other hand, the light outside blinds, that shake and rattle and bang when the stormy winds "do blow, do blow," are a fair substitute for the cooling shade of forest-trees. You may have learned that life is a succession of compromises. Building in New England certainly is. No sooner do we get nicely fortified with furnaces, storm-porches, double windows, and forty tons of anthracite, than June bursts upon us with ninety degrees in the shade. Then how we despise our contrivances for keeping warm, and bless the ice-man! We wish the house was all piazza, and if it were not for burglars and mosquitoes, would abjure walls and roof and live in the open air. Just here is our dilemma. We go "from Greenland's icy mountains to India's coral strands" and back again every twelve months, whether we will or no, and are obliged to live in the same house through it all. It's really a desperate matter. I've been to the ant and the beasts and the birds. They recommend hibernating or migration, but our wings are too short for the one, our fur too thin for the other!

Seriously, you must not forget to prepare for extremes of climate. Fortunately the walls that most thoroughly resist the cold are effective against the heat. The doors and windows—the living, breathing, seeing, working part of the house—demand the twofold provision. You must have double windows in winter, to be taken off (laid away and more or less smashed up) in summer; outside blinds to ward off the summer sun, which may, in their turn, be removed when we are only too glad to welcome all the sunshine there is. The vestibules—portable storm-porches are not to be tolerated—must also be skilful doorkeepers, proof against hostile storms, but freely admitting the wandering zephyrs. Piazzas are not so easily managed. We like them broad and endless in July and August, but the shadows they cast we would fain remove when the very trees fold away their sunshades. Often a platform, terrace, balcony,—whatever you please to call it, practically a piazza without a roof,—is the best thing to have, for this will not keep the sun from the windows, when comfort requires it may be shaded by a movable awning, and by its sunny cheerfulness it will lengthen our out-door enjoyment two or three months in the year.

You are still floundering helplessly in the kitchen. I've no doubt Sister Jane has excellent ideas on the subject,—probably knows ten times as much about it as you do. Why not ask her to arrange matters for you?

LETTER XXVI.

From Fred.

EXPERIENCE KEEPS A DEAR SCHOOL.

MY DEAR ARCHITECT: We will let the sliding-doors slide, but hold on to the bay-windows. I've acted upon your suggestion, and called on Miss Jane to help me through the kitchen. She is studying the matter and will report to you soon. Meantime, will you give directions about other inside work? I want it to be ornamental and modern in style. Shall finish mostly in hard wood,—oak, walnut, or chestnut, perhaps mahogany and maple. Please give me your opinion on that point. What do you think of graining where hard wood is not used? Shall probably carpet throughout, and hope you will not change dimensions of rooms to spoil the fit of them. What about wainscoting halls or any of the rooms? Suppose common floors will answer, and common plastering for the walls, if I paper; but shall I,—or do you recommend frescoing; and what do you say to cornices and other stucco-work?

I've no time to go over all the points in your last. Some of them seem well put, others a little wild. But I give them a fair hearing and suppose you won't insist upon my adopting them. Am beginning to think I've a good deal to learn, and ought, I suppose, to be well satisfied to learn, in some other school than that of experience.

Truly,
FRED.

LETTER XXVII.

From the Architect.

FASHION AND ORNAMENT,
HARD WOOD AND PAINT.

DEAR FRED: The tone of your last, just received, is hopeful. Conviction of ignorance is the only foundation on which Wisdom, or any other man, ever builded a house. But it must be a genuine agony, as I'm sure it is in your case; so you are forgiven for asking more questions in half a dozen lines than I can answer fully in a score of pages. Instead of taking them up separately, I might give you a chapter of first principles, hoping you would then need no special directions; but I find the value of most general observations lies, like Bunsby's, in the application of 'em. It's not enough to say, "Be honest and upright." Each particular falsehood and folly must be summoned, tried, and condemned.

You ask for a style of finish that must be ornamental and modern. But I don't understand your meaning; shall need more definite instruction. Is your house intended for ornamental purposes, as summer-houses, dove-cots, bird-cages, and the like, often are? Is it to be a museum, art-gallery, or memorial hall? Diamonds and pearls are commonly thought ornamental to those who can afford them; from pink plaster images and china vases to bronze dragons and Florentine mosaics, there is an endless variety of ornaments for domestic apartments. I've heard of a woman who was an ornament to her husband, and of a man who ornamented a whole town; but when you ask me to furnish you an ornamental style of finishing your house, I'm obliged to ask for particulars. You may have curious carvings in the woodwork about the doors and windows and on the base-boards; paint pictures, or set bright-colored tile, grotesque and classic, on the flat surfaces; cut a row of "scallops and points" around the edge of the casings in imitation of clam-shells, as I have sometimes seen; or you may build over your doors and windows enormous Grecian cornices supported by huge carved consoles,—regular shelves, too high for any earthly use except to remind you, by their vast store of dust, of your mortal origin and destiny. I hold it to be the duty of the amiable architect to carry out the wishes of his employer as far as consistent with his own peace of mind; and if you insist on having a row of brass buttons around all your casings, and setting your own tin-type, life-size, at every corner, I shall acquiesce; but my sober advice is that the interior work be simple and unobtrusive. The most perfect style in dress or manner is that which attracts the least attention; so the essential finish should not, by its elaborate design, challenge notice and thus detract from the furnishing and true ornamentation of the room. Avoid fine, unintelligible mouldings, needless crooks and quirks, and be not afraid of a flat surface terminating in a plain bead or quarter round. Stairways and mantels are not strictly a part of the essential structure, and may be treated more liberally. The doors, too, should be of richer design than the frames in which they are hung; while on the sideboard, bookcase, or other stationary furniture you may, figuratively speaking, spread yourself, always provided you do not make, in the operation, a greater display of ignorance than of sense.

Rich woodwork throughout, carved panels upon the walls, inlaid floors, and elaborate ceilings, each separate detail a work of art, intrinsically beautiful apart from its constructive use, would require a corresponding treatment in the setting of the doors and windows; but the most of what is commonly considered ornamental work, in such cases, is wholly incongruous with walls and ceilings of lath and plaster and floors of cheap boards. I know you will paste mouldy paper to the walls and spread dirty carpets on the floors (beg your pardon, I mean the paper will be mouldy before you know it, and if you ever saw a wool carpet that had been used a month without being, like Phoebe's blackberries, "all mixed with sand and dirt," your observation has been different from mine); perhaps "run" stucco cornices around the top of walls, and "criss-cross" the ceilings into a perfect flower-garden of parallelograms with round corners. But the inharmony remains all the same. Any great outlay of labor or material on the casings of doors and windows or the bases, when there is no other woodwork in the room, is surely out of place.

These are my sentiments, in general, upon the ornamental; of the merely fashionable you already know my opinion. Not that this most fitful dame has no rights that deserve respect, but her feeble light is a black spot in the radiance of real fine art. When you can give no other reason for liking what you like than that Mistress Fashion approves, beware! beware!—trust her not. The time will come when you will wish even the modest handmaiden Economy had blessed it. And if a thing is really beautiful, what difference whether it was introduced by Mrs. Shoddy last spring, or by Mrs. Noah, before her husband launched his fairy boat? Nor is fine art unattainable, even in the door-casings. It does not imply fine work. The size, shape, and position of the doors and windows, and the relative proportions of the work about them, is the first thing to be studied. Then have a care that such mouldings as may be needed are graceful, and you cannot go far wrong.

You propose to finish with "hard" wood, and ask my opinion. It depends: if it's the hardness you want, should recommend lignum-vitae and ebony; if the wood, economy would suggest that white-pine, and certain other softer sorts, be not overlooked. To answer according to the spirit of your inquiry, I should say, by all means (if you do not mind the cost) use wood instead of putty. With all respect for white paint and striped paint and all other kinds of paint, there is nothing more enduringly satisfying than the natural tint and grain of the different kinds of wood suitable for building, of which we have such great variety in style and color, from the overestimated black walnut, to the rarely used white-pine,—rarely used without having its natural beauty extinguished by three coats of paint. What I wish to say is, that finishing your woodwork without paint does not, necessarily, require the said wood to be of the kinds commonly called "hard." Any wood that is not specially disposed to warp, and that can be smoothly wrought, may be used. Those you mention are all good; so are half a dozen more,—the different kinds of ash, yellow-pine, butternut, white-wood, cherry, cedar, even hemlock and spruce in some situations. There are several important points to be religiously observed if you leave the wood, whatever the variety, in its unadorned beauty. It must be the best of its kind; it must be seasoned to its inmost fibre; it must be wrought skilfully, tenderly cared for, and, finally, filled and rubbed till it wears a surface that is not liable to soil, is easily cleaned, resists the action of moisture, and will grow richer with age. Hence, I say, by all means finish with unpainted wood, if you are not afraid of the expense, and yet paint and varnish are good, and putty, like charity, covereth a multitude of sins. Nothing protects wood better than oil and lead, and by means of them you have unlimited choice of colors, in the selection and arrangement of which there is room and need for genuine artistic taste. Yes; good honest paint is worthy the utmost respect. When it tries to improve upon nature's divine methods and calls itself "graining," it becomes unmitigated nonsense,—yes, and worse. It is one of the sure evidences of man's innate perversity that he persists in trying to copy certain beautiful lines and shadings in wood, not as an art study, but for actual use, when he may just as well have the perfect original as his own faulty imitation. What conceit, what blindness, what impudence, this reveals! What downright falsehood! Not in the painter,— O, no, skill is commendable even when unworthily employed,—but in him who orders it. You may buy a pine door, which is very well; pine doors are good; you tell every man that comes into your house it's black-walnut or oak or mahogany. If that isn't greeting him with lying lips and a deceitful heart, the moral law isn't as clear as it ought to be. You may think it's of no consequence, certainly not worth making a fuss about, but I tell you this spirit of sham that pervades our whole social structure, that more and more obtrudes itself in every department of life, comes from the bottomless pit, and will carry us all thither, unless we resist it, even in these milder manifestations, as we would resist the Father of Lies himself. Truth and falsehood are getting so hopelessly confused that we can scarcely distinguish one from the other.

One other suggestion in this connection. Without either painting or graining you may get a most satisfactory effect, both in looks and utility, by staining the less costly kinds of woods; using a transparent stain that will not conceal but strengthen the natural shading, and at the same time change its tint according to your fancy. This is an honest and economical expedient. It only requires that your lumber shall be sound, tolerably clear,—a good hard knot isn't alarming,—seasoned, and put up with care. The cost is less than common painting, and the effect as much better than graining as nature's work is more perfect than ours.

Don't ask me any more questions till I've disposed of these already on hand.

LETTER XXVIII.

From Fred.

THOUGHT PROVOKES INQUIRY.

MY DEAR ARCHITECT: In spite of your prohibition, I must pursue one or two of the inquiries already raised, in order to understand the answers given.

What is the objection to cheap floors, if they are always covered with carpets? Am I to understand that you do not approve of lath and plaster for walls and ceilings of first-class dwellings? If so, what would you substitute?

It seems much easier to say what to avoid than what to accept; but that, I believe, is the privilege of critics and reformers.

Why do you despise the modern fashions so heartily? Are the old any better?

Yours,
FRED.

LETTER XXIX.

From the Architect.

CONSISTENCY, COMFORT, AND CARPETS.

MY DEAR FRED: I don't despise the new fashions. I admire them—when they are good. Will you please try to understand that a thing of beauty is a joy *forever*? Whatever is born of truth, whether in art or religion, belongs to eternity; it never goes out of fashion. Will you also remember that modern styles, modes, fashions, inventions,—call them what you will,—are the mere average product of human thought and labor during a few years; the old that abides is drawn from the superlatively good of former countless generations, culled over and over again till that alone remains which has stood the test of your critics and reformers all along down from Adam, or up from the last monkey who wept to find his first-born without a tail and morally accountable.

Certainly it is easier to say what to avoid than what to accept, for there's more of it. Broad is the road of error, and the faults and follies, vices and sins, that wrangle and riot therein, are thicker than crickets on a sandy road in October,—thicker and blacker. You may catch them all day and there'll be just as many left. But the devoted followers of truth you may count on your fingers and carry them home in your bosom. Besides, the right thing to do cannot be told in detail for another, since every man must manifest his own individuality as he must work out his own salvation. In the millennium I expect we shall find no two houses built or furnished alike.

No; you are not to understand that lath and plaster are unfit for first-class dwellings, but there is no sense in trimming a gingham suit with point lace. A general uniformity of value in the material of which your castle is built is as essential as uniformity of style.

Yes; there is an objection to cheap floors, carpets or not; and now I've gone through your last lot of interrogation-points backward, which brings me where I left off in the former letter.

You propose to carpet the floors and ask to have them made to fit the carpets. Would you also like the walls to fit the paper-hangings, and the windows the curtains? Do you know what kind of carpets you will use in each room; just how long and how wide they will be to half an inch; the width of the borders; how much they will stretch in putting down; how much "take up" in the making (you see I can use interrogation-points)? Do you really know anything about them with certainty? I ask for information, as the same request is often made as to building the house to fit the carpets, and any attempt to comply with it seems to me a great waste of mathematics.

Concerning, the floors themselves,—leaving the yardstick out of the question,—even if they are covered by carpets six inches thick, it will not pay to lay poor ones. They should be double for solidity and warmth, well nailed for stiffness, seasoned for economy, and of good lumber for conscience' sake. Seasoned for economy, I say, since nothing is more destructive to carpets, especially to oil-cloth, than cracks in the floor underneath them. Yes,—one thing; the warped edges of the boards, that sometimes raise themselves,—that are almost sure to do so in spruce, which is never fit for floors, though often used. It's my conviction that spruce floor-boards, two inches thick and one and a half wide, would contrive to curl up at the edges. If you have good floors, furthermore, you will not feel obliged to cover them at all times and at all hazards. I remarked that the houses built when the good time coming comes will not be all alike. I can tell you another thing about them, though you may not believe it; there will be no wool carpets on the floors,—no, nor rag ones either. The people will walk upon planks of fir and boards of cedar, sycamore from the plains and algum-trees, gopher wood and Georgia pine, inlaid in forms of wondrous grace. There will be no moth or *dust* to corrupt and strangle, neither creaks nor cracks to annoy. It's a question among theologians whether the millennium will come "all at once and all o'er," or gradually. I think the millennial floors must be introduced gradually,—say around the edges,—for I do not suppose you or any one else in New England will give up the warm-feeling carpets altogether. And yet one who has seen a carpet of any sort taken and well shaken, after a six months' service, will hardly expect added health or comfort from its ministration. If your observation of this semiannual performance isn't sufficient, and you are curious to know how much noisome dirt and dust, how much woolly fibre and microscopic animal life, you respire,—how these poisonous particles fill your lungs with tubercles, your head with catarrh, and prepare your whole body for an untimely grave,—you can study medical books at your leisure. They will all tell the same story, and will justify my supposition that you will cover the floors with *dirty* carpets. Doubtless they will be shaken and "whipped" (they deserve it) two or three times a year, and swept, maybe, every day. The shaking is very well, but though it seems neater to sweep them, yet for actual cleanliness of the whole room, carpet and all, I suppose it would be better at the end of six months if they were swept—not once! For whatever can be removed from a carpet by ordinary sweeping is comparatively clean and harmless,—that which sinks out of sight and remains is unclean and poisonous.

DUST TO DUST

There are two ways of lessening the evil without exterminating the cause. One is to shut the room, never using or opening it, except for the spring and fall cleaning; the other is to lay the carpet in such way that it may be taken up and relaid without demoralizing the entire household. Talk about the carpets fitting the rooms; there should be a margin of two feet—a few inches, more or less, is unimportant—at each side. Then if you have a handsome floor, the carpet becomes a large rug—no matter how elegant—that may be removed, cleansed, and put back again every morning if you like. You may fancy a border of wood either plain or ornamental, the surface of which shall be level with the top of the carpet. This is easily made, either by using thicker boards around the edges or by laying wood carpeting over the regular floor. One caution concerning fancy floors; don't make them too fanciful. We don't like to feel that we're treading under foot a rare work of art, and I've seen certain zigzag patterns which merely to look at fairly makes one stagger. Thresholds are on the floor, but not of them, nor of anything else, for that matter, and though somewhat useful in poetry, are often provoking stumbling-blocks in practice. Necessary at times, doubtless, but we have far too many and too much of them. Even where rooms are carpeted differently they are not needed. If you must have them, let them lie low and keep dark.

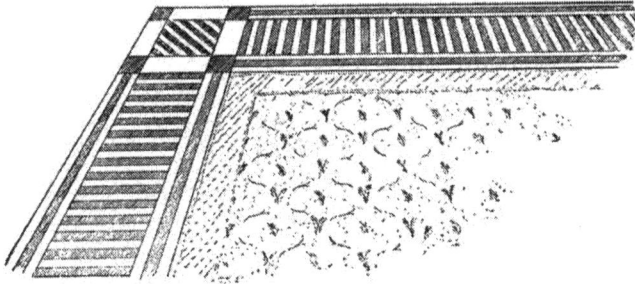

WOOL AND WOOD

If you paint or paper the walls, as you will if they are plastered, keep this in mind: the trowel finishes them as far as use is concerned. Whatever is added is purely in the nature of ornament, and must be tried by the laws of decoration. If you enjoy seeing "a parrot, a poppy, and a shepherdess," bunches of blue roses, and impossible landscapes, spotted, at regular intervals, over the inner walls of the rooms, you will choose some large-figured paper. Perhaps, if the pattern is sufficiently distinct and gorgeous, you will think you need no other pictures; and the pictures themselves will be glad to be left out if they have any self-respect. I'm sure you don't enjoy any such thing. Some of the fancy paper-hangings are artistic and beautiful in design; for that very reason they ought not to be repeated. I would as soon hang up a few dozens of religious-newspaper prize-chromos. The general effect is the point to be considered. Why not have both? Because you can't. When you have a picture so pretty and complete as to attract your attention and fix itself in your memory, the general effect is lost if you discover the same thing staring at you whichever way you turn. 'T is the easiest thing in the world to have too much of a good thing. Sometimes the better the thing the worse the repetition. This general effect which we must have is well secured by a small, inconspicuous figure, or by those vine-like patterns, so delicate and wandering that you don't attempt to follow them. Better than either are the plain tints, which give you, in fact, all you require; a modification of the cold white wall, and the most effective background for pictures and other furnishing. As much ornament as you please in the border at the top, and at the bottom, too, if the rooms are high enough. All horizontal lines and subdivisions reduce the apparent height of the room. Indeed, you may use trimming without limit, either of paper or paint, wood and gilt moldings, provided they are well used. Color, after all, is the main thing. If there is any good reason for putting this upon paper and then sticking the paper to the wall, I've not learned it. It is cheaper, cleaner, and better to apply it directly to the plastering, either in oil or water-colors. Oil is the best; water the cheapest. In any case, the best quality of plastering is none too good. For the papering it may be left smooth, but for painting, especially with distemper, the rough coarse-grained surface is very much the best. The chief objection to stucco arises from its being a cheap material, easily wrought. It is so often introduced as if quantity would compensate for quality,—a common error in other things than stucco. Though often desirable and appropriate, as a general rule the more the worse. No amount of gilding will give it anything but a frail, often tawdry appearance, that does not improve, but deteriorates, with age.

WOOD WORK ON PLASTERED WALLS

Wainscoting is always in order; it is a question of harmony, when and where to use it. What you have in mind is really an extended and ornamented base. Of course, it enriches the room, but it begins a work to which there is no limit. It should be supplemented by a corresponding wood cornice at the top of the room, and between the two as much decorative woodwork as you can afford; until "the walls of the house within, the floor of the house, and the walls of the ceilings" are carved with "cherubims and palm-trees and open flowers." A costly wainscot at the base of the walls, with paper and stucco above, seems to me a great lack of harmony. I would spread my richness more evenly. In using different kinds of wood, the raised portions, being more exposed, may be of hard varieties, the sunken portions of softer materials, even lath and plaster, which may be frescoed, covered with some rich colored plain paper, or hung with violet velvet, according to your taste and means. The old-fashioned chair-rail seems to me a sensible institution It occupies the debatable ground between use and beauty, and may therefore be somewhat enriched. The plastering beneath it may be given a different tint from that above, and when the walls are high its effect is good. It is really carrying out the idea of panelling, to which there is hardly a limit in the way of variety.

Some of your questions have led me a little way from the building toward the furnishing, but I've tried to dispose of them categorically, and am now ready for another lot.

LETTER XXX.

From Miss Jane.

AUTOBIOGRAPHY AND ARCHITECTURE, POTATOES AND POSTSCRIPTS.

MR. ARCHITECT: Dear Sir,—After so long an indirect acquaintance through our mutual friends, it is quite time we were formally introduced. Allow me to present myself: Sister Jane, spinster; native of New England, born to idleness, bred to school-teaching; age not reported, temperament hopeful, abilities average; possessor of a moderate competence, partly acquired, mainly inherited; greatly overestimated by a friendly few, somewhat abused as peculiar (in American idiom "funny") by strangers; especially interested in the building of homes, and quite willing to help Mr. Fred carry out his ambitions in that direction by any suggestions I am able to make.

SISTER JANE, SPINSTER

I've taught school, and I've taught music; sold goods in a store and worked in a factory; run a sewing-machine, travelled with subscription-books, and hired out to do house-work; and I solemnly aver that the only time I was conscious of genuine enthusiasm for my work, or felt that I was doing myself or others any actual good, was while keeping house. In school I was required to teach things I knew little and cared less about, and to punish the dear children for doing precisely what I would have done myself had I been in their places, losing all the while in amiability more than was gained in mental discipline. My experience in a factory was limited to three months. From working with the machines and as they worked, hardly using more intelligent volition than they, I began to fancy myself becoming like them, with no more rights to be respected, no more moral responsibility, and left without even serving my notice. Clerking I tried "just for fun." If all people who came to trade were like some, it would be the pleasantest, easiest work imaginable; if all were like others, the veriest torment. It was an excellent place to study human nature, but made me somewhat cynical. My sewing-machine had fits and gave me a back-ache, so I've locked it up until some one invents a motive-power that can be applied to house-work, washing, churning, mincing meat and vegetables, driving sewing-machines, and—if it only could—kneading bread, sweeping floors, washing dishes, ironing clothes, and making beds. My book agency was undertaken for the sake of travel,—of learning something, not only of the land we live in, but of its people and homes. If I had gone from house to house and with malice aforethought begged an outright gift of a sum equal to my commission on each book, I should have felt more self-approval than in asking people to buy what I had not the slightest reason to suppose they wanted.

Now I'm sure you are beginning to think me one of the disagreeably strong-minded, who think the whole world has gone astray when it's only themselves who are out of tune, but, truly, I'm not; only I don't like to be or to feel idle and useless, nor yet to be constantly striving to do from a sense of duty what is positively distasteful.

Like many other important discoveries, my aptness for house-work was found out by accident. Our next neighbor happened to be thrown, without a word of warning, into one of those dreadful whirlpools in regard to help, to which even the best regulated households are liable. My services, charitably volunteered as temporary relief, were gladly accepted, and the result on my part was two years of pleasant and profitable labor. All I earned was clear profit, and I had the satisfaction of knowing I saved the family many times over what was paid me. I'm converted beyond the possibility of backsliding to this truth: that there is no work so fit and pleasant, so profitable and improving, to the mass of womankind,—rich or poor, wise or unlearned, strong or weak,—yes, proud or meek,—as the care and control of a home; none so worthy of thorough study, none so full of opportunity for exercising all the better bodily and mental powers, from mere mechanical and muscular skill, up through philosophy and science, mathematics and invention, to poetry and fine art.

From potato-washing to architectural design the distance is great, yet there are possible steps, and easy ones too, leading from one to the other.

I began with the potatoes and know all their tricks and their manners. The accompanying sketch is the nearest approach to architecture yet attained. A long way off, you will say; but I insist it is worthier of recognition than the plans of amateurs who begin with the parlor and leave the kitchen out in the cold. It is not for Mr. Fred; he must work out his own kitchen. If Mrs. Fred can't help him, more's the pity. I give my notions of general principles; the application of them I leave to you.

My kitchen is not merely a cook-room, nor yet the assembly and business room of the entire household, as in the olden time. It is the housekeeper's head-quarters, the mill to which all domestic grists are brought to be ground,—ground but not consumed. I should never learn to be heartily grateful for my daily bread if it must always be eaten with the baking-pans at my elbow. Indeed, we seldom enjoy to the utmost any good thing if the process of its manufacture has been carried on before our eyes. Hence the dining-room is a necessity, but it must be near at hand. If the kitchen cannot go to it, it must come to the kitchen. If this goes to the basement, or to the attic, that must follow, but always with impassable barriers between, protecting each one of our five senses. The confusion usually attending the dinner-hour should be out of sight; the hissing of buttered pans and the sound of rattling dishes we do not wish to hear; our sharpened appetites must not be dulled by spicy aromas that seem to settle on our tongues; we do not like, in summer weather, to be broiled in the same heat that roasts our beef; while, as for scents, wrath is cruel and anger is outrageous, but who is able to stand the smell of boiling cabbage? Yes; the kitchen must be separated from the dining-room, and the more perfect its appointments, the easier is this separation. The library and the sitting-room are completely divided by a mere curtain, because each is quiet and well disposed, not inclined to assert its own rights or invade those of others; but the ordinary kitchen, like ill-bred people, is constantly doing both. Thomas Beecher proposes to locate his at the top of the church steeple. That is unnecessary; we have only to elevate it morally and intellectually, make it orderly, scientific,

116

philosophical, and the front parlor itself cannot ask a more amiable and interesting neighbor. As the chief workshop of the house, the kitchen should be fitted up and furnished precisely as an intelligent manufacturer would fit up his factory. Every possible convenience for doing what must be done; a machine for each kind of work and a place for every machine. Provision for the removal and utilizing of all waste, for economizing to the utmost all labor and material. Then if our housekeepers will go to school in earnest,—will learn their most complicated and responsible profession half as thoroughly as a mechanic learns a single and comparatively simple trade,—we shall have a domestic reformation that will bring back something of the Eden we have lost.

Respectfully yours,
SISTER JANE.

* * * * *

P.S.—Surreptitiously enclosed by Mrs. John.

DEAR MR. ARCHITECT: Jane has just read her letter to you aloud for John's and my benefit. John listened to the end without moving a muscle. When she wound up with the garden of Eden, he got up, took off his hat (he will keep it on in the house), made a fearfully low bow and said, "Perfectly magnificent, Jane! I begin to feel like old Adam, already." Then he burst out laughing and took himself out of the room, leaving the door wide open, of course, and kicking up the corner of the door-mat. You see he's one of those men who think home isn't home-like unless it's sort of free and easy. He'd be perfectly willing to eat and sleep and live in the kitchen,—if I had the work to do; and though he likes pretty things, and would feel dreadfully if I didn't look about so, has a perfect horror of smart housekeepers, and thinks women who care for nothing else the most disagreeable people in the world.

The trouble with Jane's letter is that she doesn't go into particulars enough, and that's why I want to add a postscript. I wish I could describe the kitchen in the house where she has been living. The people had so much confidence in her judgment, that they just allowed her to fix things as she chose, and it's really quite a study. It mightn't suit anybody else, but it shows what may be done.

She began by taking one of the pleasantest rooms in the house, although 'twas in the basement, and had windows cut to bring them on the south and east sides. Then she had an outside door at the south with a wide piazza over it, which made the room actually just so much larger. Across one side of the room is a wide stationary table,—I suppose men would call it a work-bench,—with a fall-leaf, in front of one of the windows, especially for an ironing-table. Of course it can be used for anything else. One part of it is about eight inches lower than the common height, where ever so many kinds of table-work can be done sitting. Underneath the higher part are drawers and places for all the things that are useful about the laundry-work. Her sink is in the midst of a perfect cabinet of conveniences. There's a hook or a shelf for every identical rag, stick, dish, or spoon that can be used or thought of; shelves at each side, and drawers that never by any possibility will hold what doesn't belong in them. One thing she won't have; and that's a cupboard under the sink for pots and kettles. She says it's impossible to keep such a place clean and sweet. Things are shoved into it sooty and steaming to get them out of the way, and it soon gets damp and crocky beyond all hope of purification. Hot and cold water run to the boilers and kettles, and there's a funny contrivance for sprinkling clothes. The washing almost does itself. The tubs are of soapstone, at the opposite side of the room from the ironing-table. Over the entire stove—she might have had a range, but didn't want one—there's a sort of movable cover with a flue running into the chimney that carries off every breath of steam and smoke from the cooking. One would never guess at the dinner by any stray odors. It is made of tin; the kettles boil quicker under it, and it makes the room a great deal cooler in summer by carrying the extra heat off up the chimney. She has a place for the bread to rise, and a cupboard close by for all the ironmongery belonging to the stove, zinc-cloth and blacking-brush included.

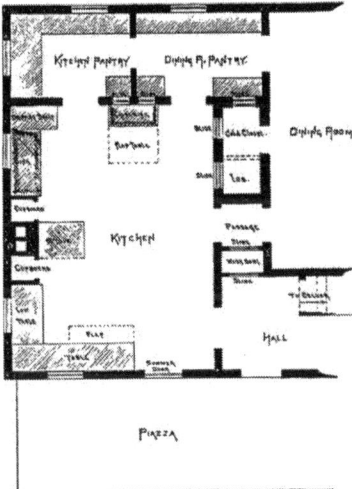

SISTER JANE'S KITCHEN

Her pantry I won't undertake to describe. It adjoins both dining-room and kitchen. John says she never does anything in getting dinner but just sit down in an easy-chair and turn a crank. That's one of John's stories, but she certainly will prepare a meal the quickest and with the fewest steps of any person I ever knew. The funniest thing about it is, that I've known eight people at work in the room all at once without being in each other's way one bit. But that's no closer than men work in their shops.

Jane intends to stay with us this winter, and I expect we shall have jolly times, for we're going to board the schoolmaster. If he calls to see you, as I think he will, I want you should read Jane's letter to him. She would take my head off if she knew I mentioned it, but I think he ought to know what's before him.

Respectfully,
MRS. JOHN.

P.S. No. 2.—Unnecessarily appended by John.

MY DEAR ARCHITECT: If we've got to go through the whole establishment on transcendental principles, I shall send in my resignation straight.

Sister Jane's a regular trump; Penelope and queen of Sheba rolled into one. But when the women-folks begin to preach, I always find it best to keep still and consider my sins. I haven't had a chance to say much lately, but I've kept up a tremendous thinking, and when I do get the floor look out for me. How do you happen to know so much about the millennium?

Yours patiently,
JOHN.

LETTER XXXI.

From the Architect.

DOMESTIC-SERVICE REFORM.

Dear Miss Jane: Your very kind letter was received and gratefully appreciated. As the world grows less ignorant and wicked, we should naturally expect missionaries and reformers to find their occupation going, if not quite gone; that modern reforms would be mere play compared with the stern and mighty movements that in former times have blessed mankind and balked the Evil One. But somehow the need for missionary work seems greater every year. We are not even permitted to go to the heathen. They come to us without waiting for an invitation; if not as pupils in the lessons of civilization, they come as teachers. Sometimes they are aliens, sometimes our own kith and kin. To keep what we have won and gain the next height requires new zeal, and ever greater efforts,—requires the very work you are doing; for a well-ordered home, though it consist of but two members, is a tremendous missionary society. The light streaming from its windows is an ever-burning beacon of safety to our most cherished social institutions.

First and chiefly, this essential home work needs to be taken from the hands of indifferent, careless servants and confided to those who realize the nobleness of the responsibility, and will strive to meet it faithfully. Ultimately, the ignorant, careless ones must be taught, but that will never be till culture is a manifest necessity and finds a fit reward. When a man undertakes the charge of a new business, he learns, not only its general principles, but as far as possible, its minutest details, otherwise he fails inevitably, and the place is given to his well-qualified competitor. If our prospective housekeepers were amenable to similar rules, the competent mistresses of this most useful art would find plenty of apprentices glad to serve them long and well for their tuition, and if those who have now the care of households will patiently instruct their help, they will find abundant recompense in a more faithful and efficient service.

Doubtless we must wait a little longer for our lost Eden to be restored by the angels of the household; but, in the hastening of that good time, such examples, permit me to say, as your own will be worth far more than any multiplying of conveniences and labor-saving machines for the benefit of those who do not know or care to learn how to use them,— examples of the nobleness, the gentility if you please, of all useful labor. Until that everlasting truth is understood and applied, there will be more need of your teaching than of my plans. If you will teach your neighbors what a fully equipped home building should contain, I will try to show them how their wants can be supplied. Teach them, at the same time, what it need not contain. As certain folks do not understand how heaven can be enjoyable without a Tartarean attachment to which all disagreeable people and performances are consigned, so a common notion of home, that earthly epitome of heaven, appears to be that it should also contain an abridgment of the same direful institution; that there must be somewhere in the house a place of torment, the angels who abide therein, giving us our daily bread and doughnuts, being of a totally different type from the glorious creatures singing songs of praise and operatic melodies in the upper stories. That the genius of the kitchen and the parlor can be one and the same is a conception too stupendous for the average understanding.

This, too, I hope you will insist upon. Every man who would build himself a house shall first sit down and—not count the cost, that comes into my department, but—ask himself solemnly what the house is for. To live in, of course. But living is a complex affair; it is constant growth or gradual death; there can be no standing still. Is the house to be an end, or a means; a help to make the life-work larger and better, or an added burden? Shall it lift, or crush him? When this solemn questioning is honestly done, we shall have a new order of domestic architecture. It may not be classic, neither Grecian nor Roman, Gothic nor French, but the best of all that has gone before and the last best thing thrown in. We shall have more cheap houses, more small ones, I think; more comfort and less show, more content and fewer mortgages.

LETTER XXXII.

From Fred.

GO TO; LET US BUILD A TOWER.

MY DEAR ARCHITECT: I've been hearing a variety of suggestions from Miss Jane, the substance of which she has already forwarded you in a letter. Her ideas are excellent. They ought to be adopted in every household. I wish to have them carried out as far as possible in mine, when the time comes. She favors a basement kitchen, which I had always thought objectionable. If adopted it would change my arrangement considerably. What do you think of it? How high shall I have the different stories, and will you give me some hints for exterior? I intended to have a tower or a cupola, but after so much change I hardly know where I am coming out. There is something very imposing about a tower, and a cupola seems to finish the house handsomely, besides affording fine views. I feel decidedly partial to French roofs, but have seen some very awkward ones that I should be sorry to imitate. They give excellent chambers and have a modern look. The latter point I suppose you will not think important.

Truly,
FRED.

LETTER XXXIII.

From the Architect.

BASEMENTS AND BALCONIES.

Dear Fred: Of course Miss Jane's ideas are good. When a woman honestly tries to understand her work and do it well, she is sure to succeed, especially in this matter of the equipments of home.

The basement arrangement depends mainly on the location. When this is favorable it is undoubtedly economical, nor is it necessarily inconvenient or unpleasant in any way, but quite the reverse. You are fortunate if your site will allow it, for it adds enormously to the capacity of the establishment. At least two sides of this lower story, "basement" you call it, should be above ground to insure dryness and plenty of light. Then all the heavier work of the house, including the eating and drinking, can be done on this floor, leaving the upper stories intact for loftier purposes. The old-fashioned cellar as a storehouse for a half-year's stock of provisions—bins, and barrels by the dozen, of potatoes, apples and cider, corned beef, pork, vegetables, vinegar, and apple-sauce—is extinct. Hence the space once thus occupied is almost a clear gain if made into finished apartments,—an economy that will commonly allow a family room on the next floor, whereby the going up and down stairs is no more serious than if both are one story higher. The sketch is an illustration of what the basement adds. The capacity of the little house is more than doubled by it, while in point of style the augmentation is even greater than in room.

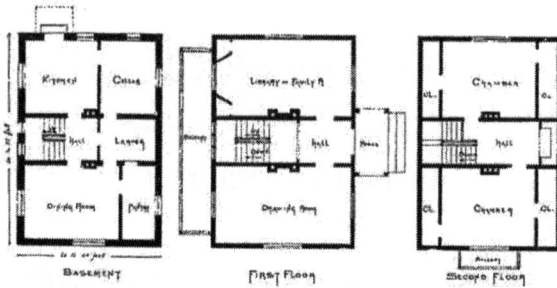

BASEMENT   FIRST FLOOR   SECOND FLOOR

WHAT THE BASEMENT ADDS

As to height of stories, you are quite as liable to make them too high as too low. For rooms within the common limits of size, ten to eleven feet in the clear is enough. Even nine is by no means dangerous. If too high for their area, they seem like large closets, giving a feeling of being walled in, hardly less unpleasant than the low-hanging ceilings of the last century. I know the argument of better ventilation. But that depends. The old, seven-foot rooms, with their huge fireplaces, big enough to hold a load of wood, ox-team and all, undoubtedly held purer air than is found in the hermetically sealed apartments of the present time, whose ceilings are out of sight.

As you say, a tower is often very imposing. It is not always certain who feels the imposition most heavily, the man who pays for it or the man who looks at it. They are not only imposing, but they contain six or seven stories, one above another, of eight-foot square rooms, deducting a Jacob's-ladder stairway at one side, whereon people climb to the topmost room for the sake of looking out in the wrong direction through a round dormer-window, scratching their heads in the mean time on the nails that come through the roof! Cupolas too are lovely,—especially on a barn,—

and top off a house in the daintiest fashion possible; just as, to set forth great things by small, the "knob" on the sugar-bowl cover finishes the sugar-bowl. Many houses do appear unfinished without a cupola, and I'm sorry for them, because when the cupola is built it looks so much like the handle on a big cover that I half expect some giant to come along and lift it off to take a peep at the curious animals underneath. For, truly, they are curious animals, and build some curious nests. I like, as well as you, to get up above my neighbors now and then, and look down upon them. I never see a tall chimney or church spire without wishing there was a spiral staircase around the outside of it, from which to view the landscape o'er. In fact, to be candid, if I had happened to live a few thousand years ago, I am afraid I should have taken stock in the Babel enterprise, not really expecting to leave this terrestrial ball in that way, but just to see how high we could go. The audacious tower of the Centennial I shall certainly patronize. But on domestic buildings, unless for better adaptation to the site, or for some special use, there are other things more to be desired than these lofty appendages. An open balcony, hanging from the highest point of the main roof, just below the scuttle, or the flat, if there is one, on the top of the whole, surrounded by a protecting balustrade, affords a better place for observation and costs less than those laborious affairs whose use and beauty often neutralize each other.

OUTLOOK FROM THE ROOF

How dare you think anything claiming to be a French roof ugly to look at? People who are fond of that style admire them from a sense of duty, because they are French roofs. Perhaps if I was a Frenchman I should like French roofs, too; being an American, I like American roofs better. You do, however, give one reason for your preference,—the complete chambers,—which is merely another way of saying you like three stories better than two,—a good argument, by the way, for the basement, which is surely more convenient than an attic. I enclose a sketch, intimating an outline and style that will suit your location. The roof, which is not French, either in form or *costliness*, will contain all the dormitories and store-rooms you can use, unless you propose keeping a three-story boarding-house.

LETTER XXXIV.

From the Schoolmaster.

FOUR ROOMS ENOUGH.

MR. ARCHITECT: Dear Sir,—Once, in conversation with you, I made some inquiries as to the feasibility of building houses, especially of brick, with reference to future enlargement. My present ambition is bounded by a house of four rooms. One in which all the household work shall be done, including the eating. It shall contain the cooking-stove, the dining-table, laundry conveniences, etc., and may be called kitchen, dining-room, laboratory, or simply work-room. An apartment to be used solely on account of its facilities for doing house-work. It should be of good size, and a pleasant outlook is desirable, but not necessary. A second room for ordinary and extraordinary use; to sit in, to talk in, to read and write and visit in; the books are kept in it, and the sewing-machine, the piano and the flower-stand, the birdcage and the pictures; a large, pleasant room, where the sunlight loves to shine in upon us and we love to look out upon the sunshine. It is parlor, library, drawing-room, living room; in fact, it is the house itself, to which everything else is accessory. A family sleeping-room, sunny, simple, and airy, and a guest-room of similar character, complete the establishment. More than these four principal rooms would be a burden, less would hardly suffice for comfortable living. The problem is to arrange a plan that shall be convenient and complete before it begins to grow, and to which future additions may be made without serious loss. I also want counsel concerning ventilation, both on general principles and with reference to the unfortunate box in which I am daily compelled to breathe my own breath over and over, variously flavored with the commingled exhalations of sixty pupils, with whom I grow cross, restless, or stupid, according to the state of the school-room atmosphere. I believe it is just as wicked to allow children to breathe impure air in their school-rooms or their bedrooms as it would be to put poison in their dinner-pails and require them to swallow it.

My friend, Mrs. John, takes a kindly interest in my quadruple plan, and assures me it will be quite sufficient for a sensible housekeeper. Do you suppose such a one can be found?

If convenient, I will call upon you in a few days.

Truly yours,
SCHOOLMASTER.

LETTER XXXV.

From Mrs. John.

CONVENIENCES AND CONJECTURES.

Dear Mr. Architect: The building-fever seems to be contagious in our neighborhood. The teacher who boards with us is the latest subject. He pretends it's all for fun, but has been studying plans for weeks, and now, after getting the advice of the entire household, is going to throw it all away and apply to you, as he should have done in the first place. I overheard him explaining to Jane how the cooking-stove is to be in a sort of recess by the chimney, with tin-lined doors to shut it out of sight; the wash-boiler at the opposite side, enclosed in the same way, and having a contrivance overhead to carry off the steam; how there are to be cupboards at each side of the wide window, making it a sort of bay, with a wood-box window-seat; how the sink is to be converted into an elegant sideboard by an ornamental cover, and everything else in the room contrived so it can be shut up or folded up out of sight when not in use. Of course Jane assists, and the combined wisdom of the two is something appalling to ordinary mortals. I should certainly think the affair was getting serious if anything of the kind ever did turn out as other folks think it ought. They are wonderfully harmonious now, but I don't believe Jane will ever be satisfied without a separate dining-room.

THE OLD, OLD STORY

John wishes me to ask what he shall do about warming his house. Says he has not decided whether to have fireplaces or stoves, grates or a hot-air furnace, steam, hot water, solar heat, or depend on a scolding wife to keep things warm.

Yours truly,
MRS. JOHN.

LETTER XXXVI.

From the Architect.

THE LESSON OF THE ICE-HOUSE.

MRS. JOHN: Dear Madam,—Without doubt the affair is getting serious, but do not give yourself any uneasiness as to the issue. The Divinity that shapes our matrimonial ends is, happily, a wiser power than that which designs our houses, however it may appear to outsiders. Your friend talks like a gentleman and a scholar. I admonished him discreetly, promised to study his interesting problem and give him a chapter on ventilation; which, by the way, is so intimately connected with warming, that I may be obliged to make a sort of company letter in answering your husband's inquiry on that subject. Tell him, in brief, to use fireplaces if he has a hundred acres of wood-land to clear up; stoves, if he can live without air; grates, if he doesn't mind the trouble and the ashes; furnace, if he can set it directly under each room and can find one that won't strangle him some windy night with poison gases; and steam or hot water, if he can run a machine-shop and keep a competent engineer. Solar heat may be more available than he thinks, but his doubt as to the last-named mode proves that he has no experimental knowledge of it. Neither have I.

Tell him also to protect his family as carefully as he protects his ice, and the house-warming will be a simple matter. The conditions are identical, only turned inside out. In one case the heat is to be kept from penetrating, in the other from escaping, and both require the same treatment; not, perhaps, to the extent of stuffing with sawdust,—confined air is just as good,—but the walls and the floors, the roofs and the windows, should be made to prevent the escape of heat. He may think I underrate his scientific attainments, but it will do no harm to remind him that an air-tight house may be a very cold one. A man would freeze to death in a glass bottle, when a coarse, porous blanket would keep him comfortable. Double windows are not to keep cold air out, but to keep the heat in. India-rubber weather-strips have, doubtless, caused ten times as many influenzas as they have prevented. More heat will radiate through a window of single glass than would be carried out by the air through a crack, half an inch wide, at the side of it.

These suggestions are "just to set him a thinking."

LETTER XXXVII.

From John.

SHINGLES, SUNSHINE, AND FRESH AIR.

MY DEAR ARCHITECT: When I stepped into the background, I didn't propose to be left entirely out in the cold. I've followed Fred through the most of his gropings after grandeur, and listened patiently to one of Jane's dignified essays on the sublimity of housekeeping; but when my wife begins romancing, and the schoolmaster is allowed to run wild, as though his moonshine was brighter than that of other folks, I think it's time to call the meeting to order.

While you have been gossiping I have been at work, and now our house is almost done,—that is to say, it's well begun. The stone walls of the first story are finished, the frame is raised and covered. I've done one thing without asking anybody's advice; covered the roof with the best cedar shingles I could find. I hired an honest man to lay them, who would throw out all that were dubious and lay the cross-grained ones right side up, and painted the tin valleys both sides before the shingles were laid. Then I took the difference in cost between this and a good slate roof and put it in the savings-bank. At the end of twenty years, if my roof lasts as long, my deposit will put on the best kind of a slate roof and leave three hundred dollars to go to the Society for the Promotion of Fine Art in General and Rural Architecture in Particular. I know the shingled roof may burn me up, if the chimney should happen to take fire some windy night, but 't won't cost so much for repairs as slate if they should blow over, either all at once, or one brick at a time. My neighbors may not like the looks, especially while it's new; but if we have nothing uglier than a mellow gray-shingled roof, I don't think anybody'll be hurt. I wish we had something like the tile roofs I've seen in foreign pictures. They'd go first-rate with my stone walls.

The eave-spouts bother me. I don't need to save the water from the roof, and have concluded to let it pour where it pleases. The porches protect the doorsteps, and I think it will be easier to take care of it after it falls than to hang gutters all around emptying at the corners and angles. They are troublesome things anyway. The leaves clog them, the ice dams them, the snow comes down in an avalanche and smashes them, they fall to leaking and spoil the cornice, and after they are all done there's no certainty that the water won't run the wrong way. I can put them up afterwards if necessary, but don't believe it will be.

The last counsel you gave me was to open the eyes of my house for the daylight to shine through without let or hindrance. I'm beyond advice on that subject. Carpets and curtains shall fade rather than wife and babies. My windows yawn like barn-doors. There isn't a room in the house that won't have the sun a part of the day, and he looks into the sitting-room from the moment his cloudy bedclothes are thrown off in the morning, till he hides his face behind Mount Tom at night. My glass bill will count up, but I'd rather pay for glass in windows than for iron in the shape of tonics.

Now, if you will settle the question of warming and ventilating you shall be honorably discharged. Don't try to show off your science by telling me how carbon, the wicked, poison stuff, is heavy, and we must leave a hole near the floor where it can run out and be coaxed up to the ridgepole after it gets cold, and then make pictures covered with arrow-heads to show how well-educated air ought to go! Talk as many gases as you please to other folks. I know two or three things for certain. Coal costs ten dollars a ton; that's one. I want just as large a house in winter as in summer; that's another. I mean the whole house must be comfortable, in shape to use when needed. I know a man will be cut off suddenly by his own breath if he has nothing else for his lungs. Mixing fresh air with it will prolong his career more or less, but it's only a question of time when he shall give up the ghost if he attempts to subsist on anything less simple and pure in the way of respiration than the out-door atmosphere. That's bad enough in some places. What I don't know and want you to tell me, is how to keep cool in summer, warm in winter, and at the same time have all the fresh air we can possibly consume. I know how to keep warm: build a tight room, keep it shut up, set a box stove in the middle of it, and blaze away. A ton of anthracite or a cord of hickory will keep you warm all winter, especially if you die before spring, as you probably will. I know how to have fresh air too: open the windows and let it blow; but unless a man lives down in a coalmine he can't well afford to keep warm under such circumstances.

I believe this question is the chief concern of builders here below, and whoever invents an economical solution of it will not only make a fortune, but he'll deserve one. Why don't you go for it?

Yours,
JOHN

LETTER XXXVIII.

From the Architect.

WHEN THE DOCTORS DIFFER.

DEAR JOHN: Your economical reasons for using shingles would justify cheap jewelry and rag carpets. Try to be consistent. I should object to slate on a log-barn or shingles on a stone-house. I hope you furnished your honest carpenter with a stout jack-knife, and required him not only to lay the shingles right side up, but to lay the upper ends close together, leaving them apart at the butt. Gutters are troublesome truly, but often indispensable; there is no resource but to have them thoroughly made. Poor ones are worse than none. Those that hang independently of the cornice are safest for cheaper buildings, but should be treated as an essential feature; that is, you should not complete the cornice without a gutter and afterwards disfigure it by a sloping spout having no apparent kinship to the rest of the finish.

The problem of warming and ventilating is easily solved for those who desire its solution sufficiently to make the necessary appropriations. One quarter of what is commonly spent for vanity and deceit will be ample. Most men and women, at least the unthinking, prefer fashionable show rather than health! A fearful statement, but sadly true. There is doubtless more danger from impure air than from cold. Our senses warn us quickly of the latter; the prompting of knowledge is needed to guard us against the former,—of a practical knowledge unfortunately rare. Men, women, and children are dying daily through ignorance and indifference on this subject. There is hardly a school-house to be found in which the murder of the innocents is not continually rehearsed, hardly a church in which the spiritual elevation resulting from attendance therein is not counterbalanced by an equal physical depression, and rarely a hall or lecture-room wherein an audience can even listen to a physiological discourse on the fatal effects of impure air without experimentally knowing that they are listening to solemn truth; while as to the dwelling-houses, the homes of the dear people, it requires no bloodhound's scent to distinguish them one from another! The moment the front door is opened to me, I am assailed by the odor peculiar to the establishment. It may be tuberoses or garlic, mould or varnish, whitewash, gas, lamp-smoke, or new carpets, a definite and describable or an indefinite and indescribable fragrance, but it is sure to be something besides pure fresh air.

SHINGLING

Let me give you first a suggestion for summer ventilation. Did you ever shingle the south side of a barn on a calm, hot, sunny day in July, thermometer at ninety degrees in the shade? Did you ever lay your hand on a black slate or tin roof exposed to the direct rays of a midsummer sun? Have you ever, at the close of some hot, labor-spent day in August, sat out of doors until the evening air became deliciously cool, and then climbed to your attic dormitory, there to spend a sleepless night in perspiration and despair, anathematizing the man who built and the fate which compelled you to occupy such a chamber of torment?

Now, there is no good reason why the rooms immediately under the roof of a house should be any more uncomfortable on account of heat than those of the first story. Nay, more, by the simplest application of common-sense, these upper rooms may be so coolly ventilated that the hotter the sun pours his rays upon the roof the more salubrious shall be your palace in the sky. And this I call a triumph of genius, making the seemingly destructive wrath of the elements to serve and save us.

M. Figuier tells us with just how many hundred thousand horse-power the sun, by the caloric of its beams, operates upon the surface of the earth. I cannot tell precisely how much force is spent upon the roofs of the houses that cover so much of the good mother's bosom in certain localities, but I know that it is wonderfully great, and that rightly controlled it will make the space immediately under these roofs cool instead of hot.

And this is the way to cause the heat of a burning sun to cool the attic chamber: Make the space between the rafters on the sunny sides of your building as smooth and unobstructed as possible. Arrange openings into the outer air at the lower end of each, simple or complex, according to your taste and ability. Provide also means for closing the same in cold weather. Be sure that these spaces, or flues, are enclosed either by lath and plaster, or by smooth boards, quite to the highest part of the roof, whether your rooms are finished to the top or not,—and provided with an abundant outlet at the top. This may also be as simple as the dorsal breathing-holes of a tobacco barn, gorgeously imposing as an Oriental pinnacle, or it may be a part of the chimney; only let it be at the very summit, ample, and so arranged that an adverse wind shall not prevent the egress of the rising currents of air. Mind this, too; it is by no means the same thing to let these flues open into a loft over the attic rooms, with windows in gables or other outlet.

Now, do you not see that as soon as the sun has warmed the flues, there will be a stiff breeze blowing, not over the roof, but really between the roof and the house, and the hotter the sun the stiffer the breeze; in the words of one who has tried it,—"a perfect hurricane." That is, the lath and plaster, or sheathing, which forms the inner roof, is shaded by a canopy of slate, shingles, or tin, and fanned by a constant breeze as cool at least as the outer air. But we can do vastly better than that. Instead of opening the lower ends of these flues to the outer air, they may be extended wherever the needs of the house require, or its construction will allow.

Let me remind you, under the head of general principles, that there is no such thing as "suction." Of course, you know it when you stop to think, but bear it in mind, and wherever the motive-power seems to be applied on which you rely to lift the column of air, remember that if raised at all it must be raised from the bottom. Maybe you will discover room for a moral here.

This summer ventilation is simple enough, and relates rather to comfort than to health. The great question in building, for New England and similar climates, is, indeed, how to keep our houses warm, and, without great expenditure of fuel, have a constant change of air. As you suggest, we have learned that wood costs eight or ten dollars a cord instead of the mere labor of cutting and hauling; hence we have shut the mouths of the old-time fireplaces, mouths that it would cost a fortune to feed. We find the value of building-timber increasing every year; so we make thinner walls, lined outside and inside with paper, and have cold houses, no fresh air, anthracite coal, and disease. Our grandfathers carried foot-stoves to church, where they sat and shivered, sometimes with the cold, sometimes at the doctrines. We have warm air and stale. Let us hope our children will have warmth and freshness for body and soul. They, in their homes, had big fireplaces, loose doors, rattling windows, cracks in the walls, and as they lay in bed looked at the stars through the chinks in the roof, or felt the snow blow on their cheeks which were ruddy with health and vigor. We have cylinder stoves, double windows, tight walls plastered and papered, and pale faces.

GOOD OLD TIMES

Yet we build and furnish more wisely than our ancestors. They ventilated because they couldn't help it, couldn't afford to build as we do, and could afford to burn an acre of woodland every year.

It is no light task you have set me preliminary to an honorable discharge. Next to theology and government finance there is no subject on which the doctors differ and dogmatize as in this matter of warming and ventilating, most of them preferring that the universe should suffocate rather than their pet theories and furnaces be found wanting. (I'm not speaking of the theologians.)

Let me restate a few general principles, simple and obvious, yet so important that we must not risk forgetting them. Air runs away with heat fast enough if allowed to move. Confined it is a more effectual barrier than granite walls and plates of steel. Hence the spaces in the wall should not extend its whole height unless for local ventilation. Cut them off surely at each floor, and as much oftener as you please; also make the floors tight and warm. Deafen with mortar if you can afford it, and do not allow the open spaces between the floor-timbers to extend unbroken through the house, or fail to close them between the rafters when the ceiling of the highest story is above the plates. If you wish to warm the entire house, it will be good economy to lath and plaster along the under side of the rafters quite to the ridge-pole. Finally put on your double windows, and you are ready for winter quarters.

In theory, the house being once warmed, the temperature within should scarcely change, even if the fire goes out. Practically, the walls cannot hold this subtile caloric, however scientifically they are padded. There will be crevices, too, though the prince of joiners builds your house, through which the warm air will escape. But replenishing this inevitable loss would be a small matter, if the breath of life were a needless luxury. Unless, however, we are willing to suck poison into our veins with every breath we draw, slow but sure,—poison expired from our lungs and emanating from our bodies, poisonous gases liberated by the combustion of fuel, poison dust and decay from the waste of inorganic material,—we must have a never-ceasing supply of fresh air around us everywhere and always. Now this incoming fluid, cold as ice, eats fuel like a hungry giant, yet we must receive it with open arms, and, as soon as fairly warmed, send it off through the ventilating flue, bearing whatever noxious elements may chance to be afloat, and, of course, much of the warmth we love and buy so dearly. We have then to supply these three sources of loss. Obviously for economy the two former must be prevented to the utmost, the latter rigidly controlled.

Thus far, except the old fogies who don't believe in ventilation, we can all travel together harmoniously. Now our way divides, the doctors begin to differ, and the patients begin to die.

The first fork is at the two modes of warming, direct and indirect. The former includes stoves of all sorts,—sheet or cast iron, porcelain, soapstone, brick or pottery, box or cylinder, for wood or coal, air-tight,

Franklin, "cannon," or base-burner, parlor cook or kitchen cook, charcoal basin, warming-pan or foot-stove,—anything in which you can build a fire. It includes open grates and fireplaces, ancient or modern, large or small; it includes steam-pipes, hot-water pipes, and stove-pipes; and last, but not least, steam-radiators, than which it has never entered into the heart of man to conceive anything more surprising and unaccountable,—flat, pin-cushiony things, big as a bedquilt, dangerous-looking hedgehoggy affairs, some huge and bungling, others frail and leaky, but radiators still. In brief, the heating apparatus, whatever it may be, stands in the room to be warmed.

By the indirect mode it is enclosed in a chamber more or less remote, commonly called a furnace, and made of brick, sheet-iron, or wood lined with tin. Into this chamber cold air is admitted from some source, and escapes by its own levity, usually through tin pipes, to the rooms where the heat is needed. Sometimes it is driven out by mechanical means.

The advocates of the latter indirect mode claim for it many advantages. It is apparently clean. There are no ashes to be taken up, no hearths to sweep, no andirons to polish, no stoves to black. One fire will warm the entire house if well arranged, and, for a trump card, there may be a supply of fresh air straight from the north pole, but agreeably warmed, constantly entering the room.

The objections are less numerous but more weighty. The liability to imperfect construction and careless management often makes a furnace, especially a cast-iron one, a savor of death unto death rather than of health and comfort; also, when we are warmed by air thrown into a room at a high temperature, and dry at that, a greater degree of heat is necessary for comfort than if our bodies and clothing absorb heat from a radiating surface. The furnace, in short, compels us to breathe an atmosphere highly rarefied. We have the most careful and competent authority for believing this to be gravely injurious.

Direct radiation from stoves, or other heating apparatus, except open fireplaces, is, moreover, economical of fuel, but, on the other hand, unless abundant ventilation is provided, the atmosphere in rooms thus warmed soon becomes unfit for respiration.

Now you may stop and think. Next time you shall have the conclusion of the whole matter.

LETTER XXXIX.

From John.

HOW TO DO IT.

MY DEAR ARCHITECT: I'm in a hurry. Let me ask you a few square questions. Give me square answers if you can; if not, say so. What kind of a furnace shall I get? I've interviewed about a dozen; each one is warranted to give more heat, burn less coal, leak less gas, give less trouble and more satisfaction, than all the others put together. I suppose you object to cast-iron, because it's liable to be heated red-hot and burn the air.

Is wrought-iron any better?

Shall I put the registers in the floors or in the partitions?

What do you say to steam?

How shall I ventilate?

Will it answer to have the ventilating flues in the outer walls?

There seems to be no doubt that the foul air should be drawn from the bottom of a room; but if it's cold, how am I to get it to the ventilator on the top of the house? If a room is as tight as a fruit-can, a chimney might draw like a yoke of oxen without doing any good, and Nebuchadnezzar's furnace wouldn't drive air into it unless, in both cases, the inlets and outlets were about equal! When I go to sleep in such a room I want to be sure the dampers won't get accidentally shut.

146

Give me your opinion on these points, but don't make a long story or a tough one. If a house is to be kept warm from turret to foundation-stone, I don't see that shutting up the spaces between the timbers would amount to much, except to stop sounds from echoing through them; but when the attic is as cold as out-doors, it's plain that the cold air will be always crawling down next the inside plastering of every room in the house if it finds a chance.

Yours,
JOHN.

LETTER XL.

From the Architect.

THE BREATH OF LIFE.

DEAR JOHN: No man ever built himself a house without getting out of patience before it was finished.

Among all the furnaces you have examined, a certain one is doubtless better for you than any other; when I find out which one, you shall be informed. Reliable testimony on the subject can only be given by some one who has tried different kinds in the same house under similar circumstances for a considerable time. As we never have two seasons alike, and do have about three new first-class furnaces every year, it is difficult to find this valuable witness. Printed testimonials are worth three or four cents per pound. I do not know that cast-iron furnaces are more liable to be overheated than others, and you cannot "burn the air" with them if they are, unless you burn the furnace too. You may fill a room with air, every mouthful of which has been passed between red-hot iron plates, not over half an inch apart, and I do not suppose the essential properties of the air will be perceptibly changed, or hurt for breathing when properly cooled.

The danger from cast-iron is in its weakness, not in its strength.

You speak of poison carbon. Carbonic acid is not poison. It is harmless as water,—just. It will choke you to death if you are immersed in it. Trying to breathe it in large quantities will strangle you. But we drink it with safety and pleasure, and may breathe a little of it, even as much as thirty per cent, for a short time, without serious harm. But carbonic oxide, which is also liberated from burning anthracite, is an active poison, and one per cent of it in the air we breathe may prove instantly fatal. Now it is fully proven that these gases laugh at cast-iron and pass through it freely whenever they choose. Wrought-iron plates are supposed to be more impervious. The popular notion that foul air must be drawn from the bottom of a room is based, I think, upon a superficial knowledge of the weight of carbonic acid, an ignorance of the law of the diffusion of gases,—upon a realizing sense of the cost of coal, and an insensibility to the worth of fresh air. Even such unreliable witnesses as our senses assure us that the air at the top of a high room— say the upper gallery of an unventilated theatre—is far less salubrious, though not overheated, than that below. We know, too, how quickly the sulphurous gas that sometimes escapes from those warranted furnaces not only ascends through the tin pipes, but rises in the open stairway if it has a chance. The hurtful carbonaceous gases doubtless go with it, and are then diffused through the room. The most forcible objection to allowing the air to escape through the ceiling is that it is a wanton waste, not only of heat, but of the fresh air that has just come from the north pole by way of the furnace and cold-air box, and which, by virtue of its warmth, goes in all its purity straight to the ceiling. Accordingly the heavy cold air lying near the floor and laden with poison must be drawn out through the ventilating flue, till the upper warmth and freshness fall gently on our heads, like heavenly blessings.

Let me digress here to answer another question. No, don't put your ventilating flues in the outer walls if you expect the air to rise through them in cold weather; for it will not, if they reach the moon, unless it is warmer than that lying at their base. You may as well expect water to rise from the cistern to the tank in the attic because the pipe runs there, as that air will rise simply because there is a passage for it. Sometimes holes are made into the chimney-flues, but this is robbing the stoves or the fireplaces. It is better to build an independent flue so close that it shall always feel the heat from the black warm heart of the chimney, for warmed by some means it must be. Yet warm air does not choose to rise. It falls like lead unless lifted by something heavier than itself.

To return to the former point. When you can warm within a ventilating flue all the air passing through it more economically than you can warm the same quantity in the room from which it is taken, then you may admit the air to feed this same flue near the bottom and perhaps save fuel; but I doubt whether the remaining air will be any purer than if an equal amount had been allowed to escape near the ceiling. The answers to your square questions necessarily dovetail. The hot-air registers should always be in the partitions if possible. It saves sweeping dust into the pipes; it saves cutting the carpets; it lessens the risk of a debilitating warm bath to people addicted to standing over them; it diffuses the heat more evenly through the room; and, owing to this better diffusion, there is less waste through the ventilating outlet at the top of the room, if it should be there.

The foregoing refers to rooms heated on the furnace principle, where all that seems needful for complete ventilation is a sufficient outgoing of the air to cause a constant change. In theory, too, the warm air must cross the room to make its exit. Indeed, the plan of admitting it at the top and drawing the cold air from the base has been strongly urged by one of the most earnest and thoughtful advocates of thorough ventilation. In practice, this fresh air is apt to come from the region of the coal-bin and potato-barrels, especially in very cold weather, and I doubt whether it will find the door of escape sooner at one side than another, unless immediately over the entrance. As to your next inquiry, I do not think our winter quarters can be warmed so safely and healthfully in any other way as by steam or hot-water radiators; but the first cost of the modes now in use puts them beyond the reach of common people, the very ones who need them most. Whether it's the tariff on pig-iron, the patent

150

royalties, the skilled labor, the artistic designs, the steam joints and high pressure, or all combined, that make the cost, I cannot say, but I have faith that some one of the noble army of inventors will, erelong, give us a system more economical in manufacture and simple in use than any at present known. It will hardly bring him a fortune, however. The real benefit to humanity will be too great for a temporal reward. Not only will this coming system be available for cheap and isolated houses, but when they stand compactly, one boiler will send its portable caloric to the dwellers on one entire square, as gas and water are now distributed.

If stoves or other local radiators are used, you must of course provide for the entrance of pure air as well as the exit of the impure. With two openings in the ceiling, the air will commonly ascend one and descend the other. Open fireplaces, whether for wood or coal, are in favor with those who have learned to love fresh air, besides being, for their cheerfulness, an unfailing antidote to melancholy, and other selfish, spiritual ills.

The truth in regard to their healthfulness is simply that they compel us to sacrifice a large amount of fuel to the goddess of ventilation, far more than would be needed to give us a better state of the atmosphere, if applied in some other way; for the fire itself is hungry for oxygen, fireplaces for wood are mightily prone to smoke, and anthracite coal releases its poisonous gases at times so rapidly that none but the most voracious chimney will carry them safely away. To answer your questions directly: with a good stove in the hall and in each of the rooms not commonly used, you would probably afford one or two open fires for those constantly occupied, and keep comfortable with less outlay for fuel than with a furnace. But you would need an accommodating fool to make your fires, and an industrious philosopher to keep them burning. In this matter of warming and ventilating the more you know the more you will wish to learn. My hope is to set you thinking and studying. Read Dr. George Derby's little book on Anthracite and Health, from which I have drawn already for your benefit; read the statistics of the increase of pulmonary diseases; get the physiological importance of fresh air so clearly before your mind's eye that your dinner seems a secondary consideration, and don't be deceived by any bigoted commentators, or forget to use your own common-sense.

While warming our backs we may dispose of some adjacent matters. You can make a very pretty fireplace for wood of the common buff-colored fire-bricks, either alone or variegated with good common red bricks; a hearth of encaustic tile, pressed bricks, or even Portland cement. Let the hearth be a generous one, two and a half feet wide, and at least two feet longer than the width of the fireplace, if you mean it for actual use. You must not suppose I object to cheap things because they are cheap and therefore common. The more so the better if they have real merit; but the marbleized slate mantels so abundant have not enough intrinsic beauty to justify them in supplanting the more honest and unpretending ones of wood. Real marble ought to be too expensive for such houses as yours.

BRICK FIREPLACE

With a furnace your house becomes a lumber-kiln, and any wood that has not been tried as by fire will, under its influence, warp and crack and shrink; in carpenters' phrase, "it tears the finish all to pieces." The rapid shrinking of the joists and studs near the hot-air pipes is also apt to cause cracks in the plastering that would never appear if the whole frame could shrink evenly, for shrink it will more or less. The application of these remarks would be, putting in the furnace as soon as possible, and keeping it steadily at work drying sap from the wood and water from the plastering till it enters upon its legitimate mission of warming the house.

When you have read all this about heating and ventilating two or three times over, these conclusions will begin to crystallize in your mind:—

Open fires give the surest ventilation and the best cheer.

If stoves are used for economy, fresh air must be systematically admitted.

Furnaces are immensely useful to warm the bones of the house and as a sort of reserve force; but the heat they give is somewhat like a succession of January thaws.

If you begin to investigate you will discover a fearful amount of ignorance and indifference where you should find positive information, and the most discouraging obscurity or conflicting statements among those who profess to be wise in such matters.

LETTER XLI.

From John.

ETERNAL VIGILANCE.

MY DEAR ARCHITECT: You did well to send the key to your puzzles, else I might have frozen to death before finding out how to keep warm. But you've earned your discharge, which I forward herewith. Now I'm going to send you some grains of wisdom, gathered during my experience in building, which you may distribute at your discretion among your clients. When a man—I don't care if it's Solomon himself—undertakes to build a house, tell him from me, to wind up all other earthly affairs before beginning; wind them up so tight they'll run for a year or two without any of his help. Then turn over a new leaf,—learn to get through breakfast before seven A.M., in order to be on the ground every moment, from the time the first spadeful of dirt is thrown out till the last touch of paint is put on. You may make full-sized drawings for him of every stick and stone, write specifications by the yard, and draw up a contract that half a dozen lawyers can't expound, there'll still be a thousand little things that won't be done as he wants them.

The openings in the basement wall somehow get out of place, an inch or two too high or too low, or at one side, then the windows over them will look askew. The air-spaces in the wall will be filled up where they ought not to be, or left out where they ought to be filled; then the frost will go through one and the rats the other. If he uses colored mortar, it will be too dark or too light, or too something,—then he'll be obliged to paint the whole wall. The drains won't be put in the right place, or they'll pitch the wrong way; then he'll have to dig out new ones. The receivers for the stove-pipes will be forgotten or set in the ventilating-flues; then he might as well have no chimney. The masons will drop bricks and mortar and trowels down the flues; then he'll have to climb upon the roof with a brick tied to a rope and try to churn them out. Just at the place where the flues ought to be plastered outside and in, against the floor and roof timbers, the masons can't reach, and like as not they'll turn a brick up edgewise if a joist happens to crowd; then his house will burn up and never give him any more trouble.

The war with the masons is short and sharp; that with the carpenters long and tedious. There are ten thousand ways you don't want a thing done, only one that suits you. Setting partitions looks like easy work; I don't believe a house was ever built in which all of them and the doors through them were in just the right places. I know they 're not in mine. I'd give three times the cost of the door if one of them could be moved, two inches, and as much more if another could be made six inches wider. I tried to have one of the mantels set in the middle of one side of the room, but somehow it got fixed just enough away from the centre to look everlastingly awkward.

The rough work gets covered up pretty quickly, but it pays to keep watch and see that the spikes are put in where they belong; that the back plastering reaches quite up to the plate and down to the sill; that timbers are not left without visible means of support, or hung by "toe-nails" when they ought to be well framed and pinned. It's hard to make a carpenter believe that plastering cracks because his joists and furrings and studs won't hang together, but it's true a good many times. You like, also, to have something more than a good man's assurance, that the furnace pipes are "all right," and will sleep better on windy nights if you have seen all exposed corners guarded by a double lining.

The gas-man had his work to do over because some of the drop-lights were not in the centre of the ceilings.

I tremble to think of what might have been if I had left the painter to his own devices. It seems very clear to say you'll have the outside painted a sort of a kind of subdued gray, with trimmings a little darker, bordering on a brown; but unless you stand over the paint-tub with a loaded revolver, you'll get anything but what you expect. It may be a great deal better, but it won't be what you wanted. By the way, there's a great responsibility resting on the painters,—I don't mean the old masters, nor the young ones either, who seem to have forgotten that outside decoration was once considered quite worthy the tallest genius,—but the more modest artisans, who call themselves house and sign painters. Their broad brush often makes the beauty or the ugliness of a whole village. I'm ready for any suggestions on the subject. Hanging the doors is another point that needs watching. They'll be sure to open the wrong way. I've had three changed already, and I'll never hang another door with less than three butts, whatever its size. I suppose they always settle more or less. Why don't the workmen make allowance for it in fixing the catches? I tremble when I think of the painters, but I rejoice at my watchfulness when I reflect on the plumbing. The chances for leaking and freezing and bursting; the hidden pipes and secret crooks that were possible and only avoided by constant oversight! Now I can put my hand on every foot of pipe in the house, know where it goes to, what it's for, and that it won't burst or spring a leak with fair usage. I don't call it just the thing to drive a tenpenny nail square through a lead pipe, pull it out, and say nothing about it. You want to be on hand, too, when the trimmings are put on, and see that they are not too high or low, or fixed so you will bruise your knuckles every time you pull out the drawers or open the cupboard doors. Speaking of cupboards, there's no end to the bother if you don't just camp down in the pantry and stay there till the top shelf is up and the bottom drawer slides in its groove. In spite of our efforts, Mrs. John says there's no place for her tallest covered dish except the top shelf, which she can't reach without a step-ladder.

You'll never know whether you are specially bright or the joiners extra stupid, but it's certain your way won't be their way, whichever is right. I say the man who pays his money should take his choice. But I haven't time to tell the whole story. It's the same thing from first to last. The only sure way of having a thing done well is to do it yourself; the next best is to tell some one else precisely how to do it and then watch them till it's done. The worst of these little blunders is, that they won't improve with age. They stare at you every time you see them, and they'll rise up before your great-great-grandchildren, monuments of your carelessness and ignorance.

I told you my house was half done when it was well begun; now that it is almost done it seems to me only fairly begun.

Yours,
JOHN.

LETTER XLII.

From the Architect.

SAVED BY CONSCIENCE.

Dear John: We are just beginning to learn the importance of color. I don't allude to the wonderful revelations of the spectroscope almost passing belief, but the new departure in the useful art of house-painting.

The old weather-stained, unpainted walls were not unpleasant to see; even the unmitigated red, that sometimes made a bright spot in the landscape, like a single scarlet geranium in the midst of a lawn, had a kind of amiable warmth, not to be despised; but there is no accounting for the deluge of white houses and green blinds that prevailed a few years ago. If nature had neglected our education in this respect we might be excused for our want of invention.

With infinitely varied and ever-changing colors smiling upon us at all times and in all places, it is blind wilfulness not to see and strive to imitate them. We need not look to the sky nor even to the woods in their summer brightness or autumn glory. The very ground we tread glows and gleams with the richest, softest tints of every hue and shade. Look through a hole in a piece of white paper and try to match on the margin the color you find. Turn in a dozen different directions, avoid the trees and the sky, and you will have, in summer or winter, a dozen different colors. Look in the same places to-morrow, and they will all be changed, an endless variety. Some one of these soft and neutral tints should clothe the body of your house. Enliven it, if you choose, with dashes of crimson, green, or even blue and gold, but use these bright colors carefully. Aim to make your house (in this as in all other respects) in harmony with its surroundings, not defiant of them. Your proffered advice shall be duly applied, for it's true that a man may easily occupy all his leisure time, be it more or less, in watching the building of his home, however carefully the work may be laid out before he begins. No two builders will interpret and execute the same set of plans exactly alike.

There are different habits of training and tricks of trade. What seems finished elegance to one is coarse awkwardness to another; and when you enter upon the more artistic part of the work, there are fine shadings impossible, even with the best intent, to any save the cultured hand and eye. The inability to perceive and therefore to bring out these delicate expressions in the execution of the work must be borne patiently. We can pardon failure when it follows an humble, honest effort.

The unpardonable sin of builders is their wilful attempt to improve the architect's design by making alterations in cold blood, through sheer ignorance and conceit. They will reduce the size of the doors and windows; substitute some other moulding for that on the drawing; or tell you they have made a bracket, or a bay-window, or a cupola, for Mr. Rusticus that looked first-rate, and advise you to have the same thing. No thought of harmony or fitness, no fine sense of a distinctive idea, pervading the whole, and giving it unity and character, ever enters their heads. Argument and persuasion are alike useless. Your only safety lies in finding some young builder, who is not yet incurably wise in his own conceit, or an old one, who has learned that, while architects are not infallible, the taste and opinions of a man who studies faithfully a special department, are entitled to more respect than even his own. As you say, these defects are commonly incurable. Neither is there any redress. The builders will either tell you they "couldn't help it," "did the best they knew how," "thought the lumber was seasoned," "understood the plans that way," or else insist that it's better so,—and maybe ask you to pay extra for what you do not like. As to your own right to spoil the house by any alterations that strike your fancy or accommodate your purse, that is unquestioned. Architects who insist upon your having what you don't want or choose to pay for, exceed their prerogatives, and bring disfavor upon us considerate fellows. *We* never try to dissuade a man from carrying out his own ideas. We only beg him to be certain that he has a realizing sense of what he is undertaking, then help him to execute it as well as we can. The more he leaves to our discretion the more hopefully do we work.

All this is too late for you, but you may pass it along to Fred, the schoolmaster, Miss Jane, and any other friends or neighbors who may be in an inquiring mood. Tell them, too, there is no safety, even with the utmost vigilance, unless every workman carries with him that old-fashioned instrument, a conscience. Give me credit here for great self-control. This is the place for some preaching of the most powerful kind, but I refrain, knowing you are too much engrossed with the finishing of your house to heed it. Do you remember how it is recorded in terse Scripture phrase that "Solomon builded a house and finished it"? Evidently the finishing was then quite as important and onerous a matter as the building. I think it is a great deal more so. The carpenters and masons, to whom you pay a certain sum of money, build it. Before they come and after they go you exercise upon it your noblest, manliest faculties. Yet it will never be done. The walls may not grow any larger or the roof any higher, but every year will add some new charm, some new grace and harmony without and within. More and more the ground around it, the trees, the walks, and the grateful soil will assimilate themselves to its spirit. More and more each article of furniture will grow to be an essential part of the home, dear for its comfort, and beautiful in its fitness and simplicity. More and more you will learn the worthlessness of boastful fashion, and the exceeding loveliness of truth.

LETTER XLIII.

From John.

FINAL AND PERSONAL.

MY DEAR ARCHITECT: We've moved in. The house wasn't done but the plastering was dry, and the paint too, what there is of it, and enough rooms were finished to hold us comfortably. Mrs. John thought we should somehow feel better acquainted if we took possession while things were in a chaotic state, before the house had a chance to put on airs, and make us feel like intruders; that it would fit us better if it wasn't entirely hardened before we crawled into it. I told her 't would be a great deal easier to wait till everything was cleared up and we could take a fresh start, but she couldn't see it in that light. Said she'd known lots of folks to be completely overpowered by a new house, and she proposed to take it while it was sort of helpless, and would be under obligation to her. It's better, too, according to her notions, to get familiar with the rooms before furnishing them, and—I've forgotten what other reasons, all good enough but not exactly correct, as I've since found out. I'd noticed some unusual and rather suggestive performances of late, but wasn't quite prepared for a request to rent the old house the very day we moved. Matters seemed to culminate one night after the schoolmaster had received your sketches and estimates for his brick beginnings. I can't say as to their merits architecturally, but they cleared one of the rough places in a certain course that never runs quite smooth. The dining-room and kitchen arrangements are all right, and the establishment is already begun. It will take all summer to finish it, and, meantime, Sister Jane will have an opportunity to reduce some of her fine theories to practice in our old cottage. Whether they will all stand the test remains to be seen. I only hope these two wise people won't pin their sole chance of domestic happiness to scientific housekeeping, and if common-sense and dutiful intentions fail, as they sometimes will, that love will come to the rescue. Fred will build next year. He 's concluded it's better to have his work well done than done too quickly.

Yours,
JOHN.

BY WAY OF APPENDIX.

A CHAPTER FROM ACTUAL EXPERIENCE.

Now you can stay just as long as you please, and I wouldn't have you feel hurried, on any account; but if you're really going to go pretty soon, I'd like to know when it's to be, so I can lay my plans accordingly."

Thus our good landlady, when we said our new house was beginning to look nearly ready for us. A most reasonable request, and we, always cheerfully responsive to such, replied, "By all means; certainly; quite right: we'll see the workmen to-day and find out just when the new domicile will be ready for us."

In pursuance of this object, straightway then we flew to the carpenter. "Tell us, O worthy master!" we cried, "when shall the new house be done?"

"Wal, let me see." And he scratched his head with the scratch-awl. "It's a'most done now. Ther ain't much more to do. We've pretty much finished up. Ther's the doors to hang and trim, 'n' the closet shelves 'n' things to fix up; the stairs ain't quite done, n'r the front steps. I d'nno; ther's a number o'little jobs 'round,—don't amount to much,—coal-bin, thresholds, and one or two things you want to change; take three or four days, I guess, if the plumbers and furnace folks get out of the way; week, mebbe."

"You think, then, by a week from next Saturday—to-day is Thursday morning—you will have everything cleared up?"

"O yes, easy!"

Alas! ingratitude is not confined to republics. We thought it a most kind and judicious thing to grant nine days, when but three or four—six at the most—had been asked. Worldly wisdom would have said, "No, sir; three days you can't have; it must all be done to-morrow night." But we are not worldly-wise; innocent, confiding, and rejoicing, we went our way,—went our way to the plumber.

"O good plumber!" quoth we, "how long will it take you to complete the work you have begun so well?"

"How long? 'Twon't take no time. Just as soon as the copper comes for the tank, I shall finish it all up. There ain't much of it, anyhow; it's all done but that."

"And when is the aforesaid copper coming?"

"When is't a coming? Any time. Shouldn't be surprised if 'twas here now."

"You can finish it then surely within a week."

"Within a week? I sh'd think likely,"—the last remark backed up by such a smile as made further question impossible.

Once more we pursued our investigating tour, saying to the prompt proprietor of the centrifugal-stove store, "Is that new furnace that is to make June of January, that never does what it ought not to do or leaves undone what ought to be done, that asks a mere handful of coal every twenty-four hours and runs itself, ready for its trial trip?"

"It is, sir."

"Registers all set and—"

"Well, no; the registers can't be set till everything else is out of the way."

"Ah, yes, of course; but 't won't take long to do that?"

"They shall all be set in the twinkling of an eye, at a moment's notice."

And now it only remained to hie away to the painter. So we hied and hailed him.

"Tell us, O man of many hues! how much time will you need to paint and stain and grizzle and grain and tint and stripe and fill and shellac and oil and rub and scrub and cut and draw and putty and sand-paper and size and distemper and border and otherwise exalt and glorify the walls and woodwork of our house, after the other workmen are through, making allowance for what you have already done and will be able to do while they are still at work?"

"I tell you what it is, Mr. Architect, it shall be done just as soon as possible. The fact is, we've got the heft of it done now. We shall follow the carpenters up sharp, and get through almost as soon as they do."

Outwardly serene, but smiling triumphantly within, we went to our daily roast-beef, and in the sweet simplicity of a blissful ignorance and a clear conscience assured our patient hostess that the dog-days and her unworthy guests should go out together. Yet we never told a lie or wilfully deceived any man, much less a woman.

But we anticipate. At the close of the third day we essayed to examine progress at the new house. As we approached, a dim and doubtful but wondrous pleasant anticipation took possession of our fancy. What if it should, indeed, be finished! The carpenter had suggested three or four days,—three had already passed. The painter was to get through *almost* as soon, the plumber would surely be out of the way, and there would be only the furnace registers. It was, perhaps, too good to be true, and we lingered to give the notion time to grow. Opening the door at last, we received something the same shock the traveller feels when he encounters a guide-post telling him the next town is half a mile farther on than it was three miles back. But we've not lived forty years without learning to bury our "might-have-beens" with outward composure, whatever the internal commotion. We remembered there was still a week, and resolved to keep a sharp lookout that no time was wasted; an idle resolution, for the workmen were as anxious to get through as we were to have them. Faithful industry and attention we may demand, haste we have no right to ask. But our men actually hurried. We were instant in season and out of season, and can testify, with both hands in our empty pockets, that there was not an hour wasted. Yet our full-blown hopes fell, as the roses fall, leaf by leaf; drop by drop our patience ebbed, till, ere the close of the week, we sank slowly down on a pile of black-walnut shavings in the calmness of despair.

To make a long story short, we gave up, beaten, trespassed a week on our long-suffering hostess, then went to visit our rich relations. They were glad to see us when we came, and wondered how long we were going to stay. We thought best to let them wonder, which they did for the space of a few weeks, when we folded our nightgowns and silently stole—not the spoons, but ourselves—away.

We mentioned the calmness of despair. From that depth it is often but a single step to the serenity of faith, on which sublime height not the wreck of matter and the crush of worlds hath power to vex or make afraid, much less a few pine shavings and the want of a little paint. Despair is never endless; it's a short-lived emotion at the worst, a selfish one at the best. Moralizing thus, it was by some means revealed to us that people are happy in paying twenty-five dollars a week at Martha's Vineyard and Mount Desert for the blessed privilege of living in unfinished and unfurnished rooms,—breathing plenty of fresh air, typhoid malaria thrown in,—and eating such food as the uncertain winds and waves may waft thither. If at Mount Desert why not at Rock Rimmon, especially as the cost is somewhat less, the fresh air equally abundant, with nothing more malarious than the pungent perfume of the pines, and all the products of the civilized world within easy reach? Moreover, our third, fourth, and fifth stories—the floor of the latter just above the ridge pole, its ceiling just beyond the stars—were, for all purposes of use and comfort, ready for occupation. So we entered, hung up our hats, and told the busy builders we had come to stay.

Which we have done; and now it's the first of October. The leaves are falling, the rooks are calling, the crickets are crawling, and the katydids are—well, squalling. There's a work-bench bigger than Noah's ark in the drawing-room, another in the library, next size larger, five tool-chests in as many different rooms, a thousand feet of lumber in the front hall, and nine hundred and thirty-seven different colored paint-pots in the guest-room,—more or less. We pry into cupboards and drawers with our finger-nails, we keep next the wall going up stairs, draw water through a straw, and to open doors we thrust a square stick through a round hole and twist and turn till the stick breaks or the door opens. Generally the stick breaks.

But we are no longer desperate. The sound of the builder's axe and hammer mingles harmoniously with the rattling of dishes and the drumming of the piano. A profound peace possesses our souls, for Nature's own infinite glory is around us, and we go from our castle in Spain to our cottage by the sea, from our house of active industry to our restful home in the New Jerusalem, with the opening and the closing of a door. We are not anxious or impatient, being well assured that steadfast industry will finally conquer and our house be finished as far as mortal house should be. Which leads us to remark just here, that a man ought never to think his house is quite complete; he will not, if he is wise, and grows as long as he lives. Our present point is the inevitable delay in the outward finishing to which home building is especially subject,—a difficulty familiar to all who have tried it, but which people cannot always get out of by jumping squarely into it as we have done.

There are various reasons for it. A superficial view of building is one. The masons are scarcely noticed before the foundation-walls are laid; the walls shoot up in a single day; the roof spreads its saving shelter as easily as though it were a huge umbrella; the windows open their eyes in new-born wonder; the chimneys breathe the blue breath of home life out into the world; the painter touches the clapboards with his magic wand; and, with one accord, all men cry out, and especially all women, "Wal, I do declare! That air house goes up in a hurry, don't it? Guess there hain't much but green lumber gone into that. Folks'll be movin' in 'n a few days. Ketch me goin' into a house like that! I'd a good deal druther live in an old house than die in a new one."

But, for some reason, the folks don't move in. Week after week passes without visible change till we hear no more of haste, but owner and neighbors grow impatient, and can't for their lives see why that house wa'n't done weeks and weeks ago! In point of fact, when it appeared almost wholly built, it was hardly begun. The work thus far had been of the sort that can be quickly executed, much of it done by machinery. Even after the plastering is dry, the floors laid, the windows in, and perhaps the greater part of the interior woodwork in place, the actual labor of finishing is but fairly begun.

Changes always cause delay more or less serious. Whoever makes alterations in his house builds four houses. There is the first doing it, which is one; then there is the "cussing and discussing," the hesitating and final deciding to make the change, equivalent, at least in time and nervous wear and tear, to the original work, which is two; the undoing is three; and the final adjusting it to your mind is four. Woe to him by whom the change cometh, but come it will. It can be wholly avoided only by having things done as you do not want them and will never be satisfied to leave them. Of course, the want of plans is a fruitful source of alterations. We are too modest and too sensible to say all plans should be drawn by an architect, but carefully prepared they must be, and, what is commonly more difficult, thoroughly understood by the party most interested, that is, the owner.

Another reason why the lengthened sweetness of finishing is so long drawn out comes from the constant increase of "modern improvements,"—accessories deemed essential to the completeness of home comfort and convenience. Nowhere is the fertility of inventive genius more apparent than in these household appliances, to all of which the apostolic injunction applies, "Prove and hold fast the good." Hold fast and be grateful, for they are the world's best benefactors whose work makes happier homes.

THE END.

Lightning Source UK Ltd.
Milton Keynes UK
UKHW01n1425200818
327513UK00003B/133/P